Gamaliel Bradford

Twayne's United States Authors Series

David J. Nordloh, Editor
Indiana University, Bloomington

TUSAS 422

GAMALIEL BRADFORD
1863–1932

Gamaliel Bradford

By Edward Wagenknecht

Twayne Publishers • Boston

Gamaliel Bradford

Edward Wagenknecht

Copyright © 1982 by G. K. Hall & Company
All Rights Reserved
Published by Twayne Publishers
A Division of G. K. Hall & Company
70 Lincoln Street
Boston, Massachusetts 02111

Book production by Marne B. Sultz
Book design by Barbara Anderson

Printed on permanent/durable acid-free
paper and bound in The United States of
America.

Library of Congress Cataloging in Publication Data

Wagenknecht, Edward, 1900–
Gamaliel Bradford.

(Twayne's United States authors series; TUSAS 422)
Bibliography: p. 209
Includes index.
1. Bradford, Gamaliel, 1863–1932—Criticism and
interpretation. I. Series.
PS3503.R2Z9   818′.5209   81-23754
ISBN 0-8057-7355-X   AACR2

For my grandson

BENJAMIN DAVID WAGENKNECHT

Contents

About the Author

Edward Wagenknecht began his academic career at his alma mater, The University of Chicago, in 1923, and though his current rating is Professor of English Emeritus at Boston University, he has never wholly relinquished teaching. His first book reviews were published when he was in his early twenties in the *Atlantic Monthly,* the *Yale Review,* and the *Virginia Quarterly Review*; since then he has written thousands more and held two literary editorships. He has also written and/or edited some sixty books, of which about one-third, devoted largely to English and American writers (Chaucer, Shakespeare, Milton, Dickens, Emerson, Thoreau, Hawthorne, Poe, Mark Twain, Howells, etc.) use Gamaliel Bradford's psychographic methods. The only man who has ever published standard histories of both the English and the American novel, he has also written histories of New England, Chicago, and the silent film. In England he published two historical novels, and he has edited the letters of Fanny Appleton (Mrs. Henry Wadsworth) Longfellow and James Branch Cabell. Among his anthologies is *The Fireside Book of Christmas Stories,* a best-seller for more than a generation. A member of Phi Beta Kappa and the Modern Language Association, he lives with his wife in West Newton, Massachusetts; their three sons are engaged, respectively, in librarianship, college teaching, and medicine.

Preface

Though Gamaliel Bradford essayed almost every kind of literary composition being practiced in his time, he owes his reputation and his claim upon reader interest almost wholly to the special form of biographical writing he called psychography, which made him, during the 1920s and until his death in 1932, one of America's leading nonfiction writers. Moreover, although his popularity was no doubt favorably affected by the extraordinary interest in biography which flowered during the 1920s, he was quite uninfluenced by such contemporaries as Strachey, Maurois, and Ludwig; so far as he was concerned the birth-to-death biographers were of interest and value only as they furnished materials for psychography. His studies in psychography receive, therefore, the lion's share of the writer's attention in this, the first published book-length study of his work. But all his other writings, published and unpublished—poems, plays, novels—are also brought under consideration, and his extensive journals and letters have been drawn upon not only in the final chapter, which is a psychograph of the psychographer, but throughout the study.

In addition to the printed and manuscript sources listed in the bibliography, I have made use of my personal knowledge of Bradford, which began in the early 1920s, when I sent him a "portrait" of the actor Richard Mansfield which I had written in one of Robert Herrick's courses in advanced composition at The University of Chicago, and in which his methods had been slavishly imitated. A warm and close relationship followed and continued until his death. He formed a most flattering estimate of my own abilities as psychographer, wrote an introduction to my first extended study in psychography, *The Man Charles Dickens,* and encouraged me in every possible way. It may be that I should still have been a writer without him, but in that event my writing career would have been very different from what it has been.

He was greatly pleased with the studies and reviews of his own work that I published during his lifetime, and on at least one occasion expressed an interest in my doing something more extensive after his death. My book is, therefore, a very real labor of love, but I have not allowed the fact that I once sat at the feet of Gamaliel to turn it into a piece of hagiography, for I knew that he would have been the first to scorn such an approach. In his own psychographs, he was concerned with only one thing—to discern and express the truth—and he could only have wished to be approached in the same spirit.

One important document, the "Autobiography," is at present missing from Bradford's papers at Harvard's Houghton Library. It was among the materials which Mrs. Bradford deposited there, but she later drew it out and apparently never returned it. If it still exists, its present whereabouts are unknown to me or to anybody at the library. In 1920, when he gave it to Ellery Sedgwick, to be considered for possible publication in the *Atlantic Monthly*, Bradford described the "Autobiography" as "very personal and perhaps almost trivial in many of its details, unless as such details may be spiritually significant. It is certainly the history of a morbid, abnormal, self-tormenting soul, and as such perhaps should not have been written. The only excuse would be that there are other such souls in the world who may get some comfort from it." That Mrs. Bradford felt these shortcomings even more strongly than he did is shown by the letter she wrote Sedgwick, in which she says she is not sure the document ought to be shown to anybody but a nerve specialist,

and even to a doctor I would point out that in Mr. Bradford's effort to be truthful, he has toppled over backwards a little in trying to portray his defects. He has left out of account his wonderful integrity and keen sense of truth. He has left out his tender and understanding sympathy which has brought countless people to him in times of trouble. He has left out his heroic bravery and courage and patience and fortitude in bearing all these physical torments from which he has suffered so pitifully.

Some time around 1950, Mrs. Bradford asked me to read the "Autobiography" and give her my opinion of it. Since I did not take notes, I cannot now remember the document in detail, but I believe that her reservations were fair and fairly stated. Moreover, I do not believe that a reader repelled by the morbidness of the "Autobiography," if that is the word to use, would get a very different impression of Bradford's personality from some of the entries in his "Journal."

Because of this book of mine, I have incurred a number of obligations and received a number of kindnesses, all of which are gratefully acknowledged here.

Houghton Mifflin Company and Harper & Row have given me permission to quote from Bradford's writings published by them.

All quotations from manuscript in these pages are made by permission of the Houghton Library, Harvard University. The librarian, Professor W. H. Bond, very graciously gave me unrestricted access to the Bradford papers, with permission to quote whatever I might need, and in the reading room, the curator, Dr. Thomas Noonan, and his assistants, Miss Susan Halpert and Miss Melanie Wisner, went far beyond the call of duty to make the countless hours I spent there between May and November 1980, a joy to remember.

At Wellesley College, Miss Eleanor L. Nicholes, in Special Collections, permitted me to examine the manuscript of Bradford's unpublished edition of two of James Shirley's plays.

At the Wellesley Historical Society, Mr. Charles P. Thomas placed all the Bradford material in the society files at my disposal.

Through the kind offices of Mr. Stephen T. Riley, the Massachusetts Historical Society supplied the photograph of Bradford used as my frontispiece.

Mr. Charles M. Getchell, Jr., of the University of Kansas Libraries, kindly sent me information about Dr. Irene Murphy's dissertation on Bradford's plays.

Finally, I wish to thank my editor, Professor David J. Nordloh, without whose kindness and understanding nobody else's would have much availed.

Edward Wagenknecht

West Newton, Massachusetts

Chronology

1863   Gamaliel Bradford VI born October 9, Boston.

1867   First removal to Grantville, now Wellesley Hills.

1878–1879   First visit to Europe.

1882   Matriculates Harvard College but withdraws after six weeks because of ill health.

1886   October 30, marries Helen Hubbard Ford.

1889   Son, Gamaliel Bradford VII, born June 18.

1892   Daughter, Sarah Rice Bradford, born July 1.

1895   First book, *Types of American Character*, published.

1904   First collection of poems, *A Pageant of Life*, and first novel, *The Private Tutor*, published.

1910   Suicide of son, August 8.

1911   Father killed by trolley in Wellesley Hills, August 20.

1912   *Lee the American*, first study in psychography.

1917   *A Naturalist of Souls*, a collection of writings arranged to show development of Bradford's psychography.

1920   *A Prophet of Joy*, most ambitious poetical work.

1922   *American Portraits, 1875–1900*, published as first of a proposed series of psychographs treating characters illustrating the whole range of American history.

1923   *Damaged Souls*, Bradford's most popular book, published, inaugurating his period of greatest success.

1926–1928   Publication of his most ambitious completed literary undertaking—*Darwin; D. L. Moody, A Worker in Souls; Life and I: An Autobiography of Humanity*—constituting a trilogy on religious faith and doubt.

1927   Daughter marries Carroll Ross, December 16.

1931   *The Quick and the Dead*, Bradford's first and only attempt to apply the psychographic method to the study of living persons.

1932   Dies April 11, Wellesley Hills.

Chapter One

Biography, Background, and Interests

Early Life

Gamaliel Bradford VI was born in Boston, in a house at the corner of Allston and Bowdoin streets, on October 9, 1863. His paternal yeoman ancestors had come from Austerfield or Scrooby in Yorkshire, and he was the sixth Gamaliel in a direct line of descent from the Pilgrim governor. His mother, Clara Crowninshield Kinsman Bradford, was the daughter of Henry W. Kinsman, Daniel Webster's law partner. The father was thirty-two at the time of the birth, the mother twenty-seven. Three years later, she was dead of tuberculosis, leaving Gamaliel and his only brother, who would follow her when he was nine, in the care of their aunt, Sarah Hickling Bradford. Though her nephew would complain of Aunt Sarah's narrow religious views, she was a remarkable woman who began the study of Greek when she was past forty, and the obituary he wrote for her is affectionate in tone. Though he did not remember his mother, he told her in an imaginary dialogue he once wrote that while his intelligence had come mainly from the Bradfords, he thought he had derived his sensibility, aesthetic quality, and humanity mainly from her.

Gamaliel Bradford V had been born on January 15, 1831, and was killed by an interurban trolley in Wellesley Hills on August 20, 1911. He was the son of the superintendent of Massachusetts Gen-

eral Hospital. In 1858 he became a partner in the banking house
of Blake, Howe & Company; ten years later he retired from business
with a fortune to devote his energies to the public welfare. He was
an abolitionist, a civil-service reformer, and a Mugwump, and he
opposed centralization in government, high tariff, and imperialism.
At the time of the Spanish-American War, when Boston was a
center of antiimperialist feeling, he was in the forefront of the opposition. He published only one book, *The Lesson of Popular Government* (1899), but he had several thousand letters in the public
press, mainly in Boston and New York, and was admired by Woodrow Wilson. He was thrice a candidate for governor of Massachusetts but never polled more than 3,000 votes.

When the son was a child, the father read him "all sorts of
charming things" and took him walking and driving, but the boy
lived "at all times in a certain dread of his irregular discipline and
his sudden thunderstorms of reproof."[1] The father's self-absorption
was "extensive, aggressive, encroaching, demanded that if you were
to come in contact with him at all . . . you were to enter for the
time into his world. . . . He never cared to enter yours, except as a
matter of curiosity."[2] As chairman of the Wellesley School Committee, he once horsewhipped a recalcitrant schoolboy, for which he
was hauled into court and fined five dollars. He loved his son and
cared for him, and it is difficult to see how the boy could have had
a literary career, or even kept himself alive, without his support,
but, cultivated man though he was, he had no understanding of nor
sympathy with his son's ambitions; what he really wanted was that
he should be a practical man of business, like himself.

In 1867 the elder Bradford bought a small, plain house, then intended only as a summer residence, in what is now Wellesley Hills
but was then known as Grantville, a division of West Needham,
in the hope that his delicate son might have a better chance to survive in country air than in the city. Later modernized and enlarged,
it remained the writer's home to the end of his life; through the
years, the view from the windows changed "from a quiet, peaceful,
elm-lined country road, where a dozen times a day some old farmer
trudged by in his buggy to a disgusting boulevard with a throng

of automobiles like black ants when you step on their hill."³ In 1919 Bradford wrote, "I never thought any place good but here. If I had to be taken away now, I don't know how I should stand it. Helen talks sometimes about going South, where I could get out a little more; but it is quite useless to talk about it to me. I shall live and die here."⁴ The house still stands at 493 Worcester Street, corner of Bradford Road, on what is now the Worcester turnpike.

During the early years, however, the boy was taken in the winter to Boston, Cambridge, even Washington, and twice, in 1878–79 and in 1887, to France and Italy. The winter of 1875–76 he lived in his Aunt Fanny's Quincy Street house, next door to the Jameses, and between 1881 and 1886 he was much in Uncle George P. Bradford's house on Prescott Street. In 1883 he spent some time in Concord, where he lived and read and wrote in the Old Manse, thrilled that Hawthorne and Emerson had done the same before him. In Europe he was homesick, though he afterwards remembered with affection much he had seen. He remembered too an evening on Quincy Street, when Henry James, Sr., had talked at length about Carlyle, and he was grateful to Uncle George for introducing him to Sainte-Beuve. His lifelong love affair with the Boston Athenaeum began almost in infancy, dedicated first to childish recreational reading, later to the cultivation of serious intellectual interests. Otherwise the Boston months were filled mostly with longing to get back to the country.

Bradford attended the Wellesley common schools "with Irish and middle-class American boys," which he felt gave him invaluable "human sympathy and insight," though in diffident or snobbish moods he could regret that he had not been taught "to speak like George Baker or Bliss Perry."⁵ But his attendance was always irregular on account of his health. In 1882 he entered Harvard and was registered for Greek, Latin, history, algebra, geometry, and physics; but he soon broke down, remaining only six weeks, during which he attended classes for only three.

After his withdrawal from Harvard, Bradford was tutored for a considerable period by Boston University Professor Marshall Livingston Perrin, but for a time his father, who apparently still maintained a Boston office, insisted on his spending about two hours a day there, so that he should "be in the way of meeting men in town, and . . . get a desirable knowledge of the world."⁶ The men in town made no impression on him, nor he on them. With Perrin, who was not much older than he was, and who testified that he had all he could do to keep ahead of him and that his pupil never hesitated to disagree with him, he got on much better. He gave Perrin credit for an excellent grounding in Greek, Latin, and mathematics, but as early as 1883 he was finding him deficient in critical power, and they had little in common temperamentally. Moreover, Perrin "knew nothing about English writing, and I had no training whatever, except what I gave myself, in the elements of composition, much less in any of the fundamentals of historical and biographical research."⁷

Love and Marriage

Bradford himself tells us that he began falling in love with girls when he was nine, but since he also says that he never even kissed any girl except the one he married, he seems to have had intimate relations with none of the others. Harriet Hubbard Ford was born in Cincinnati, May 11, 1865, and came to Wellesley Hills with her mother, a descendant of Peter Bulkeley, the founder of Concord, and two sisters, in 1875, following the death of her father, the Reverend Lucien Collins Ford. Bradford knew her from childhood and fell in love with her when they were both very young, but opposition to their wooing came from both families. As he himself ironically expressed it, his prospective mother-in-law never really took in his "remarkable personality, or . . . took it in, alas, too well,"⁸ and Bradford's father objected violently because, at the time, Helen seemed as delicate as her lover, a condition which those familiar with her impregnable health in maturity must find it hard to credit. When the boy told his father, "I cannot live without marrying, and I can marry no one but her," he received the reply, "Then you had better not live." Late in 1883, the youngster was frantic over what he considered a cold letter from her, occasioned, he thought, by his

not yet having dared, on his father's account, to declare himself.[9]
As for her, she finally made up her mind that even if Gam lived
only one year, she still wanted that year. In September 1884, they
became engaged, and on October 30, 1886, they were married.

The marriage produced two children—Gamaliel VII, born June
18, 1889, and Sarah Rice, July 1, 1892. Helen Bradford apparently
continued poorly as late as 1896, when her husband took her to
Europe for six months; this was his last extended trip anywhere. If
the financial security supplied by his father was the first piece of
great good fortune in his life, his eminently successful marriage was
an even greater one. Mrs. Bradford not only took the best care of
him in every domestic aspect; she also understood his work and had
almost as great an interest in it as he did. She once told the present
writer that not only had she never quarreled with him but had
never been so much as impatient with him, even for a moment, and
though she was one of the kindest and most thoughtful of women,
she was no sentimentalist. Late in life he wrote, "It is the infinite
perfect and sweet understanding of H. that has saved me and kept
a touch of sweetness and joy in my work."[10] When, in 1922, their
daughter left home to teach in Illinois, he found that

It leaves a great hole in our hearts, but so long as we have each other—
Oh, God, to think of the day when we shall not. I try not to think of it,
but it hangs over me like a dark cloud most of the time, such being my
nature. It seems selfish to long to go first. Yet H. could get along so
much better than I.[11]

This wish was granted. Mrs. Bradford lived until November 23,
1954, having survived her husband by more than twenty years.
With the death of their daughter, on September 23, 1972, the
family came to an end.

Later Life and Literary Career

Bradford made up his mind he must be a great writer when he
was twelve or thirteen years old. At fourteen he wrote a tragedy
which is no longer extant. The novels "Girard" and "The Reverend

Arthur Meade" followed, along with many poems; then came the early attempts at playwriting. In 1888, the *New Princeton Review* accepted his essay on Emerson, paid him eighty dollars for it, and printed it as their leading article, and in 1891 Walter Pater wrote him that he had made certain changes in a new edition of *Marius the Epicurean* in response to his suggestions in the *Andover Review*. But it was long before these successes were followed up in kind.

He did no creative work between 1896 and 1902. In 1896 we find references to his tutoring, and in 1897 he was teaching literature at the undistinguished Copley Square School in Boston and lecturing elsewhere as well. But about 1900 he experienced so serious a breakdown that he feared death or madness; this seems to have been brought on by domestic and financial problems, the strain imposed by lecturing upon one who never overcame stage fright, and his worrying himself sick over insoluble metaphysical puzzles. For about fifteen years he made no entries in his journal, and though he afterwards believed that a record of the "hell" of those years might have value, he could not bring himself to face his memories.

In 1890–91 he collaborated with Perrin in translating Heinrich von Sybel's *The Founding of the German Empire*, and in 1895 Macmillan published his first independent book, *Types of American Character*. But the *Types* did not sell, and he was unable to find a publisher for either "The Gospel of Joy" or a volume of Elizabethan studies. Bradford Torrey encouraged him importantly: "Stick to it, don't give up: sooner or later you will find your editor, as I found Aldrich, and then your way will be smooth."[12] He found that editor in Bliss Perry, who published him in the *Atlantic* during the ten years (1899–1909) he edited it, and after Ellery Sedgwick took over he became a fixture, for he filled more *Atlantic* pages during Sedgwick's early years than any other writer.

Along with unpublished materials in the Houghton Library, the literary criticism which Perry and others published testifies to Bradford's not inconsiderable talents in this field, and his capacity for technical literary scholarship is borne out by his unpublished edition of two of James Shirley's plays at Wellesley College and the 1910 article in which he examined Theobald's claim that his *Double*

Falsehood was based on a lost play, *The History of Cardenio by Mr. Fletcher and Shakespeare*, which was entered in the Stationers Register in 1623.[13]

As will be made clear in Chapter 5, Bradford's interest in charactery had long roots (at sixteen he had gone through *Chambers's Cyclopaedia*, making lists of people he would like to write about), yet his final discovery of his way was largely accidental. Having failed, as he thought, to interest publishers in his Elizabethan studies, he transferred his attention to the Civil War period, and believing that a series of monographs on some of the leading figures in that struggle might make a good beginning, he turned first to General Lee. With the publication of the papers which finally made up *Lee the American* in the *Atlantic* and elsewhere, an important man of letters had arrived. His reputation increased steadily; during the 1920s he was not only one of the most prominent magazinists in America but often found himself described as America's foremost biographer. If his sales never overtook those of Strachey, Maurois, and Ludwig, he was still quite as prominent a figure in the contemporary renascence of biography, and during his last years he had the pleasure of seeing publishers who had long been indifferent to him contending for his wares.

After the publication of *Lee the American* in 1912, Bradford's life became largely a record of his successive publications in kind. There were seventeen more volumes between 1912 and 1932, with another to follow posthumously, for he was now in full command of his instrument and in a position to draw upon the accumulations of many years of neglect and thus produce rapidly. All these books are described in detail in Chapters 6 and 7, but certain stages in the progression should be noted here. The *Lee* was complemented by two Civil War volumes, from which Bradford turned to two volumes on famous women, European and American, with *A Naturalist of Souls* published between them in 1917 to show how the psychographic method had developed out of his earlier literary studies. Though he published four volumes devoted to individuals—Lee, Samuel Pepys, Darwin, and D. L. Moody—Bradford always believed his psychographic method best adapted to briefer studies.

American Portraits, 1875–1900 (1922) was designed as the first of a series of volumes covering representative figures from the various periods of American history. *Damaged Souls* (1923) was largely responsible for his failure to carry out this enterprise in its entirety, for it was his most successful book commercially and, in a perfectly dignified and legitimate way, the most sensational, and it led to the offer of more commisions than he could possibly have accepted. *D. L. Moody, A Worker in Souls* (1927) was prompted by the interest of John Farrar, then an editor for George H. Doran, and of Barton W. Currie, editor of the *Ladies' Home Journal,* and though Currie's interest proved something of a fizzle, the result was not only the Moody but two complementary and contrasting books, *Darwin* and *Life and I*; into this trilogy the author poured the spiritual struggles and speculations of a lifetime. In 1931, *The Quick and the Dead* presented a final variation, as Bradford's first and last attempt to apply his methods to living persons.

There were tragedies in Bradford's life—the suicide of his romantic young son over a hopeless love affair with a common and unworthy woman, followed after a year by the accidental death of his father—but his greatest handicap was his chronic ill health. From this point of view, the story of his literary life is a record of heroic devotion under what most of us would regard as insuperable obstacles.

He served five years on the Wellesley School Committee and was active in the affairs of the Massachusetts Historical Society and the Boston Athenaeum. He read and evaluated books for both the Athenaeum and the Boston Public Library, and during his last years he was an editor for the Book League of America, whose program appealed to him because it offered a balanced ration of new books and old. He belonged to the Society of the Cincinnati and the Saturday, Examiner, and Maugus clubs, and received honorary degrees from Wake Forest College and Washington and Lee University. During the last year of his life he was elected to membership in the American Academy of Arts and Letters. He died, after a comparatively long illness, on April 11, 1932, and his ashes were buried in Mount Auburn. He chose as his epitaph: *A vita maiora effagitavit.*

Aesthetic Tastes and Interests

Since for people of Bradford's temperament the world within is always more important than the world without, it seems fitting to supplement the foregoing account of his life with some consideration of his adventures with literature and the arts.

If his art criticism is that of a layman, it never degenerates into either concentrating upon painting for painting's sake or admiring a picture because he happened to like the subject. Even in later years, when his back could not stand more than ten minutes at a time in a gallery, that ten minutes could still be heaven, and among the artists who spoke to him importantly were Titian, Bellini, Luini, Carpaccio, Correggio, Memling, Cranach, Frans Hals, Constable, Van Dyck, Corot, Rousseau, and D'Aubigny. But the two painters who meant most to him were Botticelli, whose *Primavera* and *The Birth of Venus* he thought the most wonderful pictures in the world, and, in the sharpest possible contrast, Rubens. Surely his description of the *Venus* deserves to be remembered along with Pater's writings in kind:

The face of the Venus is the most marvelous, perplexing thing. It has not one shade of mythological beauty, nothing of the perfection which Raphael or Tintoretto would have given it. It is a sad face, a bewildered face, an earnest face, full of question as to why she, a pale, poor woman, like other women, is given such strange, magical power over life and death. The faces of Raphael's beauties have no puzzle in them, no question, just a supreme mastery of the divine force of beauty. But this Venus knows that she controls the world and less than anyone else can she understand why. Now how much of all this do you suppose Botticelli had in mind when he created her? Very little, perhaps. Yet surely he must have understood that she was not the typical Venus of the Greeks. Do go look at her again. And then look at the Spring beside her, which has the same subtle mystery, as if the beauty of this world were not only a divine delight, but an inexhaustible teasing perplexity —as it is—to those who take it so.[14]

With music he got further, for though he called himself "a wretched amateur" the piano was a delight to him during most of his life. There is even one amazing entry in his "Early Journal" in which he records a magnificent idea for a symphony in E flat about the fall of the Titans and maps out the movements, though he knows he could not compose the symphony, and as late as 1923 he tried unsuccessfully to set some of his own lyrics to music.

He had marked likes and dislikes, but he seems to have cared most for the baroque and classical composers. In general he disliked "program music," resenting the need for "an assiduous comparison with the program, with the use of the most wretched verbiage to elucidate the music."[15]

There are a few references to his pleasure in songs sung socially, and in youth he tried to take part in such singing, in his own opinion unsuccessfully. But, to his way of thinking, the words never had a chance against the music, and this pretty much ruled out opera. Yet he adored Gilbert and Sullivan, and such works as *The Chimes of Normandy* and *Boccaccio*, even when played on the piano, gave him "a mixture of delight and agony, the long-fled memories of things that never happened, of longings and aspirations the utter impossibility of satisfying which in this world or any other makes me so constantly yearn for death."[16] Symphonic music gave him "a dim, elusive, bewildering, enthralling suggestion of a vast possibility of ecstasies," but he could not follow nor analyze the themes, and he wondered whether others really understood and responded to music more fully than he did or whether they only pretended to.[17]

Bradford knew that in moments of real ecstasy music may surpass even literature, but simply because of the naked emotionalism of its "sweet compulsion," such responses were far more hopelessly dependent than anything readers know upon the listener's mood. Moreover, such experiences often involved "a dissipating, dissolving passion, a haunting, exhilarating, exasperating ardor, which elevates the spirit beyond hope, and then leaves it pale, exhausted, discontented, skeptical, with a grief for which it finds no obtainable remedy and no specific cure."[18] Certainly Bradford's own highly emotional approach to music must have influenced what he believed about it. To him, musicians were always a race apart, lacking positive qualities; it was hard for him to realize that a musician might have brains. "Of all the arts I cannot but think [music] the most unhealthy, at least in its modern forms."[19]

Theater came closer to Bradford than music, not only because the drama is a part of literature but because he himself aspired to success as a playwright. His first play was *Macbeth*, with Janauschek, at the Globe in Boston, in 1875. He saw Duse, Mary Anderson, Adelaide Neilson, Irving and Terry, and their contemporaries, and even met Bernhardt at a reception in 1896 and shook her hand, which he thought "not particularly clean"; she seemed "much more coarse and ordinary and more like what she is than I thought she would be."[20] In 1896 he was president of the Playgoers Club, and he read plays aloud with friends all his life; in his youth he even appeared in a Wellesley production of the *Elektra* of Sophocles. In later years, he does not seem to have attended the theater often, but the fascination never died.

He grasped the potentialities of the cinema earlier and more clearly than many of his generation. His fullest and most considered expression of his response was made in a 1921 letter in which he speaks of the movies as

an art in themselves, neither exactly pictorial nor exactly literary, but fusing the two, together with music, in a vast world of aesthetic possibility, the outer veil of which has hardly been lifted. What has impressed me most has been the extraordinary mobility, which is so utterly denied to the regular stage. The Greek and French classical drama, by accepting this limitation and making the best of it, produced the highest art form which I suppose the theatre is capable of. The Elizabethans rebelled and attempted to be mobile, with the sole result of childishness. The real stage must be in the main static and only on that condition can one get real spiritual movement. But here come these Movies, with their extraordinary versatility extending even to the portrayal of shifting states of mind, and at once open a world of dramatic devices never dreamed of before. . . . It does seem to me that I see an infinite field in which real dramatic and emotional genius has the most magnificent results before it.[21]

Elsewhere he speaks of the "strange force of illusion" possessed by the screen, "less artistic than that of the regular theatre because much more vividly real, but proportionately more overwhelming." This gave it the power "of taking you out of yourself, which is the greatest thing that life can do for us, and is at the same time the most damnable comment there is upon life." And these things often moved him to both laughter and tears in the darkness, even while he was cursing himself for a fool because he was thus moved.[22]

All in all, however, he would seem to have applied less system and intelligence to his study of the cinema than to anything else that ever interested him. Apparently he never went to the movies at all until 1921 and then confined himself to Saturday afternoons in Wellesley Hills, where he had a fatal facility for running into cowboy films. The only titles he mentions are *The Last of the Mohicans, Conrad in Search of His Youth,* and *The Covered Wagon,* which he did not like. He did not like Harold Lloyd or "Buster Keating" either, and he was completely blind to Chaplin. Once he says he would like to see some of the Griffith and German films, but apparently he never did. He knew who Mary Pickford and Lillian Gish were, but there is no record of his having seen them. Indeed, he thought all the actresses looked very much alike, and on the one occasion when he seems to have been impressed by an actress, he could not remember her name.

Books

Though books were the unfailing blessing of Bradford's life, he sometimes perversely declared that reading, like drugs, was a bad habit, which kept people from leading normal lives, and that since there were too many books already, the making of more should be prohibited and punished. He read with phenomenal speed—the 400 pages of Wilbur C. Abbott's *Conflicts with Oblivion* in an hour and a half and a long novel in galleys which he read and wrote his opinion of for the Book League in two hours—but he could read only in complete silence and solitude. In the contemporary field he always felt that even if he ran as fast as Alice, he was still falling behind.

He loved diaries and letters and, less predictably, scientific books, accounts of travel, and biographies of practical men, but he also had marked dislikes: short stories, historical novels, especially those which dealt with ancient Rome, fairy tales and the supernatural, and he was opposed to translation, committed to the extreme view that if you could not read a writer in the original, you must let him alone.

But what he loved best was to read over and over the beloved books that had long been a part of his life. He read, as he lived, by the clock, and he read, according to an elaborately arranged system, sometimes only fifteen minutes or four pages of something before going on to something else. On September 2, 1919, he read of the fall of Dido in the *Aeneid*, half a volume of Henry Adams's history, some pages of the *Troades* of Euripides, some of Voltaire's letters, a scene from *The Honest Whore*, some Sainte-Beuve, and some Shakespeare, both unspecified.

When Bradford entered high school in Wellesley, the curriculum "comprised four years of Latin, three years of Greek, two or three years of French or German, geometry, several consecutive courses of general and English history, and English literature and composition from beginning to end."[23] In 1929 he wrote, "I read seven languages with considerable facility and I have made it a rule to drop the dictionary almost at the start, and acquire by a process of gradual divination, *never* translating, but always reading in the language itself." In 1920 he told M. R. Werner that he had tackled Russian some time ago, but given it up because he was "too old and needed the time for other things."[24] He began modern Greek and Portuguese virtually on his deathbed, to fill up empty time.

"I do not mean to let a day pass without some Greek and Latin," he wrote the classical scholar E. K. Rand in 1925, "but if I had my way, I should fill the days with practically nothing else."[25] Sometimes he affirmed Greek superiority even to Shakespeare. In Latin literature, he speaks most of Virgil, admitting the weaknesses of the *Aeneid* but reading it again and again. He did not care greatly for Horace, but he appreciated and had a certain temperamental affinity with Lucretius.

About German literature he says little, though the influence of Heine is evident in his poems, and in his youth at least he was devoted to *Wilhelm Meister*. In general, however, he thought German, Italian, and Spanish fiction much inferior to French and English. Zola's "infinite pity" and "dumb grandeur" moved him,[26] but he did not read Proust. He loved French poetry, and Senancour fascinated him as he had fascinated Matthew Arnold. He began Molière when laid up with a cold at fourteen and read both him and Racine again and again. He enjoyed Dumas *fils* and Augier, but it was his relish of the plays of Meilhac and Halévy and of Flers and Caillavet that amounted to a passion.

Bradford's father read the great English and American writers aloud to him in his youth, and he continued reading aloud to his own children. As a boy, he also read Alger, Oliver Optic, Mayne Reid, Elijah Kellogg, and Henry Seton Merriman for himself; for the last two he never lost his taste. Though he professed to hate the Middle Ages, he loved Chaucer. Shakespeare he adored but deplored crying down his fellow dramatists. Jonson he could take or leave, but Fletcher was almost an obsession with him, and surely Davenant has had no more ardent modern admirer. He says little about the seventeenth century, and no other eighteenth-century writer meant anything like so much to him as Sterne, in whom he found an affinity with his beloved Shakespearean fools.

With the Romantics he came alive again. Te be sure, he rejected Burns, which was in line with his odd prejudice against popular balladry, but he adored Shelley, not for his "stability or nobility," in which he was surpassed by Keats, but for his "peculiar unearthly charm" and "seductive spiritual grace, and above all an undeniable sincerity and an ethical quality, which rather take him out of the ordinary categories of moral judgment"[27]—yet he was sufficiently Victorian to rule out *The Cenci* because of its subject matter. He never lost his admiration for Scott, though as early as 1884 he was aware that he was out of tune with the modern spirit.

Bradford's prejudice against nearly all the Victorians except Arnold and Trollope dated back to his youth, and Dickens and Browning seem to have been the ones he disliked most. Even when he admits Browning's resemblance to Sainte-Beauve in his devotion to the study of human beings, he must add that verse, not prose, was his proper medium because it helped him conceal his commonplace thought. Yet one wonders whether there may not have been some deliberate perversity in Bradford's anti-Victorianism. In 1883 he spoke admiringly of Thackeray and George Eliot; in 1897 he praised *The Woman in White*; in 1929 he mentioned Mrs. Oliphant and Mrs. Alexander nostalgically.

He was not much more sympathetic toward contemporary British literature. He admitted Shaw's brilliance but never really liked him,[28] and he took a dim view of Pinero and Jones. In 1928 he spoke of planning to read Sheila Kaye-Smith, Rebecca West, and *The Forsyte Saga* without expecting to like them. He was too sensitive a reader not to be impressed by Virginia Woolf's *To the Lighthouse*, but he wondered whether the writer should not "imply and suggest these processes, rather than develop them so confusingly and elaborately." She was not "in any way setting down actual experiences of her characters" but "simply objectifying her own experiences in similar situations and transferring them to others."[29]

Among the "classical" American writers, his debt to Emerson was the greatest.

Between 1882 and 1884 he practically made my life over, opened reaches and depths of spiritual splendor, as Matthew Arnold had done to some extent two years earlier; but as no one has even begun to do since. I cannot bring myself to go back to either Arnold or Emerson, because I know that now I should read them and judge them with stupid earthly criticism, as I do many others who do not mean anything particular to me. I am not willing to dash the glamor and the glory of that departed inspiration.[30]

Even in his youth, however, he thought Hawthorne much more of an artist than Emerson. Poe he gave credit for "intellectual passion" and power to touch "the abstract aesthetic sense" but questioned his ability to reach "the depth and warmth of human sympathy." Yet he took up "spiritual and especially intellectual problems, with such intense ardor of investigation, as if the whole welfare of his soul

depended upon the solution of them"; in this sense, Emerson himself
was far more of a "jingle man" than he.[31] Outside of Emerson, Bradford thought Whitman on the whole the most important figure in
American letters, but seldom read him because he preferred a definite
metrical form. In a way, he had the same reaction to Emily Dickinson, but he also felt "the hopeless commonplace" of his own verses
compared with "the sky-rockety, planetary vehemence and abrupt
splendor" of hers.[32]

His judgments of Frost and Robinson were probably affected by
his personal relations with them. He liked Frost's poems better,
though he denied him "intellectual depth or power."[33] He appreciated Robinson's skill and liked him personally, but thought him too
much like Browning to rouse enthusiasm. "After Amy Lowell and
the author of Waste Land and Carl Sandburg, and all the rest, I
should find rest in even Excelsior and the Wreck of the Hesperus."[34]
He long refused to read John Brown's Body "from the pitiable but
perhaps human instinct which dissuades me from all successful
works of contemporaries as being likely to throw my own into the
shade." After meeting Stephen Vincent Benét and liking him, he
was rather ashamed of this, but he still did not think Brown great
poetry.[35]

He was inclined to be severe in his judgment of contemporary
fiction, his general criticism being that all the writers lacked humor.
He was very hard on Edith Wharton and thought Dreiser and Lewis
captured only the surface. Yet he wrote "fan" letters to Katharine
Fullerton Gerould (Lost Valley) and Margaret Prescott Montague
(Deep Channel). He was shocked by James Branch Cabell's Jur-
gen, not only because he thought it indecent but because of what
seemed to him its philosophical nihilism. Yet, even though he hated
both allegory and the Middle Ages, he found it "an extremely
original and beautiful book, of a high and singular imaginative
quality," with a "haunting, dreamlike beauty of style and general
tone."[36]

Like Mark Twain, he greatly admired George Ade, and he judged
E. J. Rath "by far the cleverest and most brilliant writer of light
fiction in this country."[37] But his most surprising enthusiasm was

that for Edgar A. Guest, to whom he not only sent a birthday greeting but whom he also defended against Harriet Monroe in *Poetry*. Guest, he argued, touches the heart "in a fashion quite out of the reach of most of the estimable writers who adorn your pages." He imparts something "of the sweet, high consecration of rhythmic ecstasy to the common things that make up the daily experiences of millions of readers."[38]

In early days, Bradford called Montaigne's essays and Burton's *Anatomy of Melancholy* the most fascinating of books, but in later years detective stories moved up into this place. "For detective stories count in my life, more, I sometimes think, than even my own glorious productions. That half hour in the evening before I go to bed, what can match it?" And he told Stanley Rinehart that "the writers of mystery stories are benefactors of humanity. All other authors, chiefly myself, are only to be tolerated."[39] Once, when he went on for an hour and a half, in order to finish a book, he dreamed all night "of murders, assassinations of my neighbors and best friends, etc."[40] He was a great admirer of Edgar Wallace, to whom he wrote that his books, like H. de Vere Stacpoole's and Victor Bridges's, and unlike Oppenheim's and Fletcher's, were literature.

Bradford admired and praised the Shakespeare criticism of Edgar Elmer Stoll, encouraged M. R. Werner, and was much too easy on Paxton Hibben, Herbert Gorman, and even Van Wyck Brooks, though recognizing that the preconceived thesis became a force for distortion in such books as *The Ordeal of Mark Twain*. He never clearly explained his contempt for the More-Babbitt school of criticism. He found Parrington's *Main Currents in American Thought* "a cloudy, ill-planned, and consequently ineffectual book," which sacrifices "all impartial study of the individual to ... partisan considerations," and Beard's *Rise of American Civilization* caused him to wonder why "people are permitted to make such books at all, or any books but mine."[41]

As a reviewer Bradford was notably gentle, but though he might omit strictures and reservations, he never awarded any praise he did not mean. A close and expert student of prosody, he was frank and specific in his comments upon poems sent him for evaluation. He

told the Century Company of one novel that though it was "powerful, original, dramatic," it was also "exceedingly hideous and repul-
sive" and Doubleday that he hated another: "I realize that it is just
the sort of book the young person of today apparently likes and it
drives me to lunacy because I cannot in the least appreciate why she
likes it."[42] Even John Farrar was told of one biography that it was
"wretched sentimental rubbish which you can probably sell and
ought to be ashamed to publish, if publishers were acquainted with
such a thing as shame."[43]

Chapter Two
Poetry

Poetry was Gamaliel Bradford's first and dearest love. He was only nineteen when he wrote that if he could not be a great poet, he expected either to commit suicide or die mad. He did none of these things, but before the year was out, he had produced nearly two volumes of short poems, was working on the narrative "Bertha" and the poetic drama "Bacchus and Ariadne," and was planning another narrative, "Angelica," a comedy in the style of Aristophanes, and the novel "Girard." Even as late as 1920 he wrote a correspondent that he thought of his prose as merely a means of making people read his poetry.

His verses divide themselves into two classes—lyrics and narratives. He got two collections of the former into print—*A Pageant of Life* (1904) and *Shadow Verses* (1920)—and one long narrative, *A Prophet of Joy* (1920). Most, not all, of the narratives are early. Lyrics he continued to write, with certain hiatuses, throughout his life (by 1928 he counted well over 2,000), the only important change being that, as he grew older, he ceased to write about the historical and cultural themes he had treated in his early sonnets and concentrated on personal interests, reflections, and emotions. In the first section of this chapter, *A Pageant of Life* will be treated independently and *Shadow Verses* in connection with the vast body of unpublished material in Houghton from which its contents were drawn. Section 2 will deal with the narratives, of which the *Prophet* and "A Humble Saint" are the most important.

Lyric Poetry

The first and principal section of *A Pageant of Life* comprises a series of fifty-five generally excellent sonnets, devoted to outstanding figures, aspects, and movements of the Ancient World, the Middle Ages, the Renaissance, and more recent times. There are four other sonnets, not in the "Pageant of Life" series, nine items under the heading "Songs and Lyrics," two translations from Leopardi, and a section containing the Prologue and Songs from one of Bradford's plays, "A Mad World."

In the sonnets the octave is rhymed *abba abba*. The rhyme scheme in the sestet varies, but a rhymed couplet at the end is avoided. Among the subjects are Theocritus, Hannibal, Lucretius, Virgil, Lucian, Marcus Aurelius, St. Anthony, Julian the Apostate, *Daphnis and Chloe*, the troubadours, the Crusades, the mendicant friars, Petrarch, Chaucer, Botticelli, Cervantes, the Pilgrim Fathers, Calderón, Voltaire, and Kant. The sonnets attempt to present both the point of view of the subjects treated and the impression they make on the poet. Perhaps the most significant, in view of the author's own interests and ambitions, is

THE ELIZABETHAN DRAMA

> Land of my first love, garden of my heart!
>   Let other nations keep their simpler fare;
>   Let Spain exult in Calderon's sweet air;
> And Athens triumph in her tragic art.
> For throb of human life, for rushing dart
>   Of passion, like the storm in speed and glare,
>   What other nation can with you compare,
> Land of my first love, garden of my heart?
> Laughter and tears in like profusion come,
>   Blossom of rose, blossom of bitter rue,
>   Words which assuage the anguish they impart,
> A tongue supreme, to me the tongue of home—
>   Sweet fate, to walk through life alone in you,
>   Land of my first love, garden of my heart.[1]

The passionate sonnet on "The Renaissance" does not quite prepare us for the eager acceptance of the "no spirit world"' of Rubens: "Thine is a world of flesh,/Fresh glowing, panting, with the throb of fresh,/Intense delight of sensual joy." "The Return to Nature" laments that now that we no longer see the "omnipresent Deity" in nature, man stands "unpitied, loveless, and alone," much as in Arnold's "Dover Beach." In view of the horror Bradford felt of Bryan in 1896, "The Socialist-Idealist" is surprisingly sympathetic, and "Sainte-Beuve" expresses the ideal of the psychographer-to-be:

> To feel what other men feel; to command,
>   With insight keen, the subtle human soul;
>   To be one's self yet see what thoughts control
> The artist's brain, the soldier's gleaming brand;
> To pray with saints, yet press the sinner's hand,—
>   This was thy hope, this was thy constant goal,
>   One word will sum thy life up round and whole:
> "All longings fail save that to understand."

Yet the sonnet ends with the admission that this alone is not enough to "help the throbbing pulse to live,/Nor cheer the fainting heart, when it must die."

Shadow Verses,[2] which contains seventy-one brief lyrics, took its title from *The Duchess of Malfi*:

> In what a shadow, or deep pit of darkness,
> Doth womanish and fearful mankind live?

It was Bradford's own opinion that his poems were a franker and more intimate expression of his own personality than his prose, and that, compared to the "extreme breadth of sympathy with all moral and spiritual earnestness" in his psychographs, they were "colored by a tone of depression and sadness."[3] He was amused when one lyric, "The Clergyman," proved too shocking for *Snappy Stories*, whose editor, an intelligent young woman whose tastes were not those of her readers, admired it but did not dare to print it:

> She took him for a clergyman,
> And trusted him a lot,

> Alas, before the day was done,
>   She found that he was not.
> His face was full of dignity,
>   His garb was shaped with art,
> But she concluded God and he
>   Were rather far apart.[4]

He touched all the great themes of lyric poetry—nature, love, death, and God—and he admitted that many of his verses expressed moods rather than settled convictions. But they deal more with human relations and personal joys and sorrows than with the world without, and more of Bradford's joy in the beauty of nature went into his journal than his poems.

Some poems stand out as distinctly different from the rest, a few in form, others in character. There is an "Ode to Thomas Jefferson, Written for the Centennial Celebration of the University of Virginia." There are two satirical, comparatively long poems, written for the election of 1920, pretty scornful of the candidates, though not of the prospects of democracy, and there are musings in the same form over the Pilgrim Tercentenary and other public themes. There are also, in Volume VI of the "Poems" in the Houghton Library at Harvard, a number of pieces more or less in *The Child's Garden of Verses* tradition, expressing the point of view of both boys and girls —a bit surprising from a writer who did not greatly enjoy the company of children. Perhaps the most imaginative is "The Spelling-Book":

> The spelling-book once gave a dance,
>   And all the words careered:
> How little if and but did prance
>   And the long legged things I feared.
>
> The polysyllables went mad,
>   With such a fearful clatter!
> Like sister's talk which sometimes dad
>   Calls words with little matter.
>
> I thought the thing would burst itself;
>   But when I turned in bed,

> The book lay quiet on the shelf;
> The dance was in my head.[5]

There is also, in Volume III, a whole series of poems, illustrating how the born writer makes use of all the elements of his experience, however painful, about his son's tragic death. Though it is never named directly, the inspiration must be perfectly clear to anybody who knows the circumstances.

> I stood by his grave;
>   But he was not there.
> "If Christ can save,"
>   I cried, "oh, where
> Is my loved one now?
>   Shall I see him again?"
> And hope's buds grow
>   From the roots of pain.
> But life is strange,
>   And death, still more.
> In a world of change
>   We peer before,
> And stagger and grope
>   From grave to grave.
> And the buds of hope
>   Are all we have.[6]

There are more poems about love, however, than any other subject, and some of these are autobiographical. Every year on her birthday, Bradford addressed a poem to his wife. Here is the 1928 offering:

> The world is but a mass of vague
>   Disaster that we flee;
> But I can tolerate the plague,
>   If I abide with thee.
>
> We linger in a lovely spot
>   And yet that spot would be

A simple hell, if I could not
  Abide in it with thee.

I hardly think that I should care
  For immortality;
But how could I be anywhere,
  And not abide with thee.[7]

There is also a touching memorial poem to his sister-in-law, Harriet
Ford Cutler:

The spring, with sunlit green, again
  Enchants each vale and hill,
Enchantment wrought for thee, in vain,
  Lie still, my Love, lie still!

A thousand bursts of music throng
  The woods, as ne'er before,
Thy heart must echo to that song
  No more, ah, nevermore.

The ample splendor of the wave
  May quiver as it will,
But thou, within thy grassy grave,
  Lie still, Dear heart, lie still![8]

Most of the love poems, however, are purely imaginary. More
deal with kissing than with any other aspect of love-making, but
closer contacts are not wholly ruled out.

I confess, I shrank before,
  Duty, honor, trust forbidding.

But thy kisses charm me so,
  They would shake a will far firmer.[9]

and, better yet:

We will open the gates of delight.
We will rove the wide fields of desire.

> And the wearisome world
> Like dead leaves shall be whirled
> In our passion's devouring fire.[10]

The poet can cry:

> O God, from this burden of flesh
> Who shall deliver and save?
> We walk in the devil's mesh
> Blindly from birth to the grave.[11]

He can warn of the dangers of passion:

> Love will have his way
> Rule as lord and master,
> Though he bring his prey
> Ruin and disaster.
>
> Eyes that he doth blind
> Cannot read their sentence,
> Till they wake and find
> Life one long repentance.[12]

But prudence, too, has its dangers:

> Carry coyness not too far,
> Cunning, chaste delay,
> Lest I see you as you are,
> See, and turn away.[13]

And sometimes it even seems that disaster may be worth embracing:

> If we only lived with virtue,
> We should miss a vast amount,
> And the pleasures that might hurt you
> Are too often those that count.[14]

There are even poems in which love is regarded with a blunt cynicism:

> Yes, I may have loved thee once, my sweet,
>   I do not know,
> Cast immense desires at thy feet
>   Long ago.
>
> That is all behind now. What's before?
>   I do not know.
> I was cured of loving any more
>   Long ago.[15]

and again:

> Madonna, those days are all over,
>   I smile at my wooing so hot.
> You may wish you had called me your lover;
>   But I, I am glad you did not.[16]

Finally, in Bradford's poems, there is the ever-present thought of
God, always longed for, but never possessed. Unquestionably "Exit
God" is the best known of all his poems:

> Of old our father's God was real,
>   Something they almost saw,
> Which kept them to a stern ideal
>   And scourged them into awe.
>
> They walked the narrow path of right
>   Most vigilantly well,
> Because they feared eternal night
>   And boiling depths of hell.
>
> Now Hell has wholly boiled away
>   And God become a shade.
> There is no place for Him to stay
>   In all the world He made.
>
> The followers of William James
>   Still let the Lord exist,
> And call Him by imposing names,
>   A venerable list.

> But nerve and sinew only count,
>   Gray matter of the brain,
> And an astonishing amount
>   Of inconvenient pain.
>
> I sometimes wish that God were back
>   In this dark world and wide;
> For though some virtues He might lack,
>   He had His pleasant side.[17]

But "God" cuts deeper:

> Day and night I wander widely through the wilderness of thought,
> Catching dainty things of fancy most reluctant to be caught,
> Shining tangles leading nowhere I persistently unravel,
> Tread strange paths of meditation very intricate to travel.
>
> Gleaming bits of quaint desire tempt my steps beyond the decent.
> I confound old solid glory with publicity too recent.
> But my one unchanged obsession, wheresoe'er my feet have trod.
> Is a keen, enormous, haunting, never-sated thirst for God.[18]

Narrative Poems

When the publication of *A Prophet of Joy* had been arranged for, Bradford, with self-mocking irony, "in view of the great and enduring triumph" anticipated, gathered into one manuscript volume called "Octaves" "all my early experiments with the octave not included in the separate volume of 'Early Sketches of Percival.'" Many of these works are fragments, and none seem to call for much discussion here. Perhaps the most interesting is "Angelica," begun in 1883 but not completed until January 1887, about a girl who becomes a nun without having a vocation. Having been seduced by a lover in gardener's dress, she is dragged back to the cloister. Her lover is tortured to death, and she is finally buried beside him. The author judged this poem a close imitation of Keats's "Isabella," and in some respects not greatly inferior. But though it contains much good verse, it lacks the intensity which the subject demands, and the tragic ending is insufficiently prepared for. "Lamia," which is in heroic couplets and undated, is an attempt to improve upon Keats's treatment of the same story.

This brings us to what Bradford considered his major poetic enterprise, perhaps his supreme work, *A Prophet of Joy*. Though it was not published until 1920, there were three earlier versions, two in prose and one in verse. It is a kind of novel in verse, on the model of the long narrative poems of Byron and his contemporaries, written in iambic pentameter eight-line stanzas, rhymed *abababcc*, of which there are 567, divided into six books. Lo, here, as Chaucer would say, "the forme":

> Miss Theodora Perkins was unwed
>   At thirty-five, yet delicately charming,
> An idle and bewitching life she led,
>   And thought love's snares perhaps somewhat alarming,
> In earlier days she had been city-bred,
>   Then bought a country place, and played at farming,
> Had hens and cows but did not milk herself,
> Nor touch the polished pans upon the shelf.[19]

Bradford feared he would be accused of imitating Byron, but he told William Lyon Phelps that John Fletcher had been more important to him, and it is clear that Cervantes also contributed.[20] Perhaps his own best description of the poem was made in a letter to Ellery Sedgwick:

Meanwhile, I amuse my leisure in what you will no doubt consider the singularly futile diversion of composing a vast narrative, semi-epic, semi-humorous poem. It is something I have had in mind and worked over at odd times for thirty years, a long story of an enthusiastic youth who preaches an inspired gospel of joy to a cold world and in doing it meets with many strange characters and singular adventures and is loved by many women and finally gives his life for his cause and in the long process of his history touches all phases of our complicated modern life, Bolshevism and Christian Science and Christian sacrifice and capital and compromise and politics, all in a broad and light and laughing way, but with love and sunshine and without satire or bitterness.

At least I would have it so, and I am weaving it all in octave stanzas after the fashion of Byron and the great Italian epics, and it is an endless amusement and distraction to me and would probably be an endless weariness to everybody else.[21]

Percival Smith, a millionaire's son, starts out, Don Quixote–like, to teach men how to enjoy life. He stays for a time with Miss Theodora, a distant cousin, who half falls in love with him and from whom he takes french leave with her purse, after which he falls in with one Jarvis, whom he encounters, with two girls, in an amusement park. He meets Morgan, a reporter, addresses a meeting of radicals, and embarks upon a high-flown romance with a film actress, Aurelia McGoggin. Aurelia's aunt and her brother, Slippery Bill, burn Jarvis's books in imitation of Cervantes. Percival is taken to a Christian Science meeting, where he addresses the worshippers. After having been introduced to Ezekiel Waters, an apostle of violence, he is caught in a police raid on an anarchist meeting, but Aurelia pleads for him and he is discharged. Theodora tries to interest him in a fair but rich and fickle cousin, Cecilia. He falls in with Peter Scrimp, a multi-millionaire, speculates in Zona Oil, and becomes a director. Stocks crash; he is persuaded to go into politics and is elected. There is a strike at Scrimp's factory. Percival pleads with the men to avoid violence and is warned off by Waters. He refuses to leave, faces the mob, and is killed. Aurelia vows to carry on his work.

From this incomplete summary it may be seen that *A Prophet of Joy* has a very wide range and touches a variety of American aspects and concerns. Charles Wharton Stork called it the most important book of verse since *The Congo* and *Spoon River Anthology*, and William Lyon Phelps found it an original contribution to literature, resembling nothing else that had been written in America. But Barrett Wendell, who read it with care and admired it in many aspects, thought the treatment too genteel, and Bradford at least half agreed with him.

I appreciate fully what you mean about the lack of boldness and freedom. The thing should have more of a large vigor and sweep of

movement, should appear to pour and really should pour out a fullness
and abundance of life which should suggest much wider possibilities
behind it than could be crowded and compressed into any such com-
pass. And the Bohemian world should be rougher, more eminently and
intimately alive. I felt the need of this and hoped I had got it by suggestion at least, but I can well understand that I haven't.[22]

Perhaps. Or perhaps Wendell was asking for a different kind of
poem. One cannot but wonder whether an admixture of the kind
of realism he desired might not have vitiated the fundamental idea
of a lighthearted crusade in the interest of joy.

As usual, Bradford's own attitude wavered. He was enraptured
when he reread the second canto, and he said of the octaves that
they "writhe like serpents, and glitter like stars, and rattle and
clatter like mad castanets."[23] Perhaps he was only half satirical in
looking forward to the day when his poem should be established
"as one of the humorous classics of the world" and editors would
study the earlier versions "as they gathered up the early drafts and
paralipomena of Faust." On the other hand, though he was sure
the *Prophet* ought to sell as well as *Spoon River* and *North of
Boston*, in his heart he thought a sale of 300 to 1,000 copies more
likely.[24] The fundamental weakness of the poem is that it is not
sufficiently of a piece, and the tragic ending comes as a shock. The
light, almost flip tone of the earlier portion is simply junked, and
the work is not sufficiently focused so that one can be quite sure
just what the author was trying to say.

Though the *Prophet* was not a commercial success, Bradford
wrote one more long narrative poem, "A Humble Saint" (1923), in
iambic pentameter couplets, "a psychological study of a religious
tragedy in the Vermont hills, something no human being will ever
publish or read, but the kind of thing I like to do."[25] Compared to
the *Prophet*, it is a somber work, closer in spirit to "The Reverend
Arthur Meade" and *Between Two Masters*, and this time there can
be no question as to unity of tone.

Eleanor Hammond, a visitor in rural Vermont and a seeker who
has not yet found her way, sets out to ensnare the Reverend Simon

Styles for a lark. Styles discusses Eleanor with Miriam Bayne, one
of her fellow boarders at Miss Burham's, who thinks his harsh creed
belongs to the past, to which he replies that

> God's splendor burns with every rolling year,
> No matter who would bid it disappear.
> The past? There is no past. Eternal might
> Fixes the rolling world's deceptive flight
> In one vast continuity of God.

Simon and Eleanor's friend Roger Withington agree that she is

> No normal, wise, sane creature, shot all through
> With sunshine, like that pleasant Miriam Bayne;
> But one born mad for ecstasy or pain,
> Rapture of heaven or sharp stab of hell.

When Simon finds Eleanor lost in a snow storm and brings her
home, she talks defiantly of the storm she lives in. She cannot tell
"whether she wishes to drag him down to hell,/Or soar into
heaven." He tells her that God cannot be possessed "save by your
own immediate inward touch" and that she must either surrender
to Him or depart. But she replies that she cannot

> climb those arid heights alone,
> Or make my small way to that golden throne,
> You might have saved me, you, you might have set
> This little palpitating heart of mine,
> Where it would ever glow and throb and shine
> Among ten thousand perfect stars in heaven.
> You did not. And you may not be forgiven.

Deeply moved by a sermon of Simon's, Eleanor wrestles with God
in the woods.

> She knew now what she sought was this content,
> To let strife go, all vain, perplexed desire,
> And fall back with a sigh upon that higher,

Purer, diviner, unimagined might,
Too great for sound, too excellent for sight.

Eleanor and Miriam commend Simon to each other, but Simon
wishes only to win Miriam for God, not for himself, and Roger,
who had tarried in Vermont for Eleanor, now finds himself drawn
to Miriam, who admits that she cares for him. Meanwhile, Eleanor
longs for Simon but feels sure he is not for her:

by force of being all
God is too near to nothing. Great and small
Are easily confused in the divine.

Finally, Eleanor leaves Simon, trusting only in God to show her
the way:

The path that I must go
Is one that even you have never trod,
A path through the wide wilderness to God.
His hand will hold me, his support sustain,
Guide me through regions of untrammeled air,
Up hills of hope, down valleys of despair.
Why, God is with me, Simon, never yet
Have I faced life so much without regret.

If, as Phelps believed, *A Prophet of Joy* is unique in American
literature, what shall be said of "A Humble Saint"? Certainly there
are not many such records of spiritual seeking and struggle.

Coda: On Bradford's Poems

There are so many contradictions and so much self-mockery in
Bradford's comments on his poetry that it is hard to believe he ever
arrived at a settled evaluation of it. Intellectually he was sure that
the practically universal view that he had talent as a biographer but
not as a creative writer was probably correct. Yet hope refused to
die. "But when my prose has made my reputation," he wrote in
1922, "I have an intimate confidence that my verse will in the end

come to stand as high, or higher,"[26] and though Ferris Greenslet thought his lyrics too personal for general appeal, their author hoped they might still have value as the record of "the development of a soul."[27] "I believe still," he wrote in 1930, "that I have written songs that deserve to rank with the great lyrics of the world."[28] Yet he could not but remember that that was what Robert Southey had thought about his verses also.

When Katharine Lee Bates asked him to read his poems before a small group including Alice Brown, Josephine Preston Peabody, and perhaps Robert Frost, he refused, but his ambitions revived when Charles Wharton Stork devoted a number of *Contemporary Verse* to them. Both *A Pageant of Life* and *A Prophet of Joy* were published at his own expense, and he toyed with the idea of other subsidized publications. When Stork suggested to the Yale University Press that they bring out *Shadow Verses*, he was sure they would refuse, and when they not only accepted the book but the staff went about the office quoting from it, he was elated and dreamed of another collection next year and "A Duchess of Dreams" after that. The admiration which both Stuart Sherman and Barrett Wendell expressed for *Shadow Verses* set him up notably, and when Miss Bates got a long article about the *Prophet* and his work in general into the Boston *Evening Transcript*, he read it and re-read it and went to bed at 9:30 to lie awake until twelve with "fragments of the article and fragments of the Prophet chasing each other" through his head.[29] He even had an amusing correspondence with the somewhat crusty editor of *Poetry*, Harriet Monroe:

I relish having you refuse two or three of my poems once a year or so; it gives a fillip to the zest of life. And if you should ever accept one, I should gasp with huge astonishment to think that I had managed for once to flame up out of the fatal marsh of mediocrity in which Mr. Guest and I—and some others—usually wallow with strange contentment.[30]

The lady does not appear to have capitulated, but she was rather amiable for her; she cannot have had many correspondents who were at once so stubborn and so agreeable about rejections.

There can be no question as to Bradford's immense cleverness and fecundity in poetry, and perhaps his characteristic note is strongest in those poems in which he achieves a surprising, sometimes illuminating, slightly cynical twist in the closing verses. Rhymes chased themselves without let or hindrance through his head; he wrote verse as easily as prose, and everything was poured out *mit einem Gusse.*

This gift was not an unmixed blessing, however; like the gifts of the fairies, it imposed conditions. Bradford certainly wrote far too many lyrics, playing infinite variations upon the same theme and expressing the same idea hundreds of times. He himself once wrote:

> A multitude of songs will come
>   Upon me in the night.
> If out of all the number some
>   Were good enough to write!
>
> And some have speed and some have flow
>   And some perchance have wit
> But not a single one, I know,
>   Is really exquisite.[31]

However this may be, he was simply not the kind of writer who can spend hours or days over a lyric, polishing it to an impossible perfection. And perhaps the first lesson a critic must learn is that every artist must be permitted to create according to the bent of his own temperament and in obedience to his lights, without our insisting that he must work in another way or like somebody else, and that otherwise he will not be able to create at all.

Chapter Three
Drama

Bradford attempted dramatic composition in both prose and verse. *Unmade in Heaven* was the only play ever to see print, and none was ever acted. In this chapter, the verse plays will be considered first.

Verse Plays

The earliest plays in verse are "Bacchus and Ariadne" (dated 1883–84) and "A Mad World" (1888–89). "Hermione" (1892) was never finished. "Bacchus and Ariadne" is an imitation, with variations, in blank verse, of the classical drama, and "A Mad World," which uses both verse and prose, follows Elizabethan models very closely. The setting is an English country town during the reign of King James I, the material is divided into both acts and scenes, and there are many songs.

In a note written on May 8, 1920, the author himself described both these works very fairly:

"Bacchus and Ariadne": For a boy of nineteen to attempt a romantic-lyrico-allegorical drama, which should combine the merits of *Faust* and *Prometheus Unbound*, was sufficiently presumptuous. I was aware of the presumption and went at the work with what modesty I could. Of course the result has no final value, or perhaps interest for anyone but the author; but the blank verse is good in spots and there are passages of dramatic movement.

"A Mad World": With an erratic method of procedure outdoing even
its Elizabethan models, and an obvious imitativeness both in character
and incident, it has, I think, real touches of Elizabethan imagination,
often suggestive of Beaumont and Fletcher at any rate. I should be perfectly willing to have it printed now, though any attempt to revise it
would be hopeless.

"Bacchus and Ariadne" is in three acts, each of which opens
with a Chorus, except that what the Chorus was to say at the beginning of Act II was never written. The play begins before King
Minos's palace in Crete. The nurse recalls the conquest of Greece
by Minos, who placed the Athenians under obligation to send seven
youths and maidens each year to be devoured by "the black fiend he
hides within these walls." Theseus, who tried to deliver Athens,
is now a prisoner in Crete, where Ariadne, daughter to Minos, has
fallen in love with him. She gives him a thread to guide him to
and from the Minotaur in his labyrinth and agrees to flee with him
if he conquers the monster. While he is accomplishing this, the
Chorus tries to dissuade her but fails. Upon his triumphant return,
the lovers flee while the Chorus laments Ariadne's sin and promises
punishment.

In Act II, on Naxos, Theseus describes the glories of Athens to
Ariadne, who has an ill-divining soul. Bacchus arrives, disguised as
an old woman; he warns Ariadne and is driven off by Theseus. But
while Ariadne sleeps, Theseus deserts her and returns to Athens.

In Act III, Silenus and Triton prepare for Bacchus's formal coming to Ariadne. He tells her that he has long loved her and that it
was he who led Theseus to the Minotaur and both of them to
Naxos. Ariadne leaves Naxos with Bacchus.

"A Mad World" is a complicated and somewhat confusing pot-
pourri of Elizabethan, or rather Jacobean, themes and motives. Peter
Earwig is a self-serving Puritan who seeks to prevent his daughter
Prudence from marrying the cavalier Edgar Woodvill and to marry
her to Nathaniel Yellowshanks, a debt-ridden hypocrite who is interested only in her father's money. Sir Anthony Truepenny is an
obvious descendant of Falstaff; his daughter Marian loves Mortimer

Lackbrain, but swears she will not marry him unless he stops drinking. An Elizabethan type Clown weaves in and out of the action, involved in the various intrigues. Finally Prudence is delivered to Sir Anthony, who plans to turn her over to Woodvill, but the cavalier shows himself an honorable man by refusing to take her without her own consent. In the end, Earwig, whose eyes have at last been opened to the worthlessness of Hollowshanks, agrees to the union of Prudence and Woodvill, and of course Sir Anthony consents to allow Marian to wed Lackbrain.

The three later verse plays are much better. In "A Duchess of Dreams," which was entered, along with "A Fool and Her Money," in a Poetry Society contest of 1920, Lorenzo, Duke of Urbino, sends his envoy, Rodrigo, with the latter's friend Rolliardo, to woo Leonora, Duchess of Ferrara, as his proxy. Leonora, resentful of being thus looked over, exchanges roles with her waiting woman Mariana. Rodrigo and Leonora fall in love, as do Rolliardo and Mariana. When the Duke arrives, he understands the situation, and after considerable parleying at cross purposes, gives his blessing to both pairs of lovers.

The fable here is clear and straightforward, and the play is in rather free blank verse, divided into five acts, without scenic divisions. There is no prose, save in one letter which is read, and there are many interpolated songs by Fantaste.

Both Leonora and Mariana have considerable charm and would afford the right actresses good opportunities. Bradford's beloved Fool character is doubled in this play.[1] The real Fool is Fantaste, but Rolliardo is cut from the same bolt of cloth. Fantaste states the Fool's point of view to the Duke in Act IV:

> We fools, at least in motley, have wit enough
> To manage all men's matters but our own.
> We can conceive long plans, lay cunning plots,
> Emit sage saws with solemn utterance,
> But then there comes some sudden freak, some whim,
> And all at once we turn life upside down
> And revel in the wreck with frolic laughter.

"A Fool and Her Money" is very different, an attempt to write a modern comedy in blank verse. The scene is "a large western city," the time "the present," and the inspiration came from Fletcher, whose *Chances* furnished the epigraph:

> Familiar language, fashioned to the weight
> Of such as speak it.

Emma Hart is an oil heiress, a kind of rough diamond, who decides to test her professed admirers by pretending to be ruined. The lovers are Nathan Page, a banker; Alonzo Peters, a journalist; Leonard St. George, a lawyer; and Lemuel Stott, a theologue. Lemuel is the only one who passes the acid test, but it does him no good, for, in the third and last act, Emma decides she is too good for him and accepts St. George instead. The plot is unraveled at the end of Act II, where Emma describes her experiment to her lovers: "I've lost, not money, but *you*." As might well have been expected after this, the last act is rather confused; there is much coming and going and a juggling of ideas and standards in somewhat Shavian fashion but without Shavian skill. As often with Bradford, the characters are somewhat unconvincingly frank in explaining their motives. The blank verse is graceful enough, but it would probably neither add to nor detract much from the effect of the play in performance, for, as so often happens with T. S. Eliot's verse plays, the audience would probably miss the beat much of the time.

"Ravenac" is probably Bradford's best verse play, since, though no better done than "A Duchess of Dreams," it deals with larger and more vital matters. Henry, the old lord of Ravenac, is a strong character, and Isabel of Magny is a good study in temperament, a sophisticated woman, technically virtuous, who enjoys seeing men at her feet. That she fascinated her creator is made clear by his frequent use of her in the "Haunted Biographer" dialogues.

When the play opens, Ravenac is facing an attack by the Magnys. Lord Henry is old, and the only hope for deliverance lies in Gaston of Greille. But Gaston loves Lord Henry's granddaughter Bertha, who loves Gilbert, son of the peasant woman Martha, her old nurse. Lord Henry commands Bertha to wed Gaston, and even the despairing Gilbert agrees she can do nothing else. But the Fool Trollo tells of Gaston's past involvement with Isabel of Magny, whom he forsook when he saw Bertha.

In Act II, Isabel comes to Ravenac to see her rival, encounters Gaston there, and upbraids him. In Act III, Ravenac orders an immediate marriage between Gaston and Bertha, who swears she will kill herself rather than obey him. When he finds Bertha and Gilbert together, Lord Henry first threatens to kill the lover, then satisfies himself by banishing him.

In Act IV, Gilbert grows suspicious of Bertha, and upon her positively refusing him, repudiates her as a woman disgraced and vows vengeance upon Ravenac. He also considers returning to Isabel, who refuses to believe evil of Bertha and tells Lord Henry he is worth a dozen Gastons and that some day he and Bertha will look down from heaven upon her and Gaston "floundering in hell." Bertha and her sympathizers now send Trollo to fetch Gilbert back to Ravenac. In Act V he returns, but so do Gaston and his forces. The play ends in an orgy of slaughter; even Trollo is killed, but not until after he has had the satisfaction of stabbing Gaston.

The blank verse in "Ravenac" is very good, but Isabel is brought into Act II somewhat awkwardly, and it is not quite clear what Gilbert's return in Act V could have been expected to accomplish. Though there may be some question whether it has been led up to with sufficient intensity, the slaughter at the end is well managed, and the way the Fool is drawn into the action, vindicating his loyalty and paying for it with his life, is effective. Trollo's songs, in the Elizabethan manner, are also very good.

> Oh, bury me under the red rose tree;
> For life was a frolicsome thing to me,
> Without desire, without regret,
> And what I did with it I forget.

Prose Plays

The early prose plays require little comment. On "Tennis Balls"

and "A Love Knot" (both dated 1895), Bradford himself helps us
with a note written in May 1924:

The play ["Tennis Balls"] was, of course modeled closely upon the
French; the dying scene in the last act upon Camille and Frou-Frou.
Maurice Dearborn was a sort of replica of the choric commentators of
Dumas fils. The dialogue is heavier and stiffer than I afterwards came
to command, but has I think some elements of power. And the conception of Belle Sanders, with her ingenious scheme of revenge and its
psychological working, was entirely original with me, and still seems
to me effective and to offer acting possibilities.
    A Love Knot was written hurriedly, with the idea of supplying some-
thing after the fashion of Sardou's melodramas that could be acted by
Fanny Davenport. Much of the action is extravagantly impossible. But
the dialogue seems to me excellent, and the characters of Domenico
and Leonora are powerful and practical, unless I am completely mistaken.

    "A Roman Holiday" and "The Cracking of Thorns" (both dated
1895) were later rewritten as novels, the former as *The Private
Tutor*, the latter under its original title. (The novels are both considered in Chapter 4.) "The Bicycle Belles" (1895), an obvious
offshoot of the cycling craze of the 1890s, is a broad farce which
has no value save to show Bradford's familiarity with the popular
theater of the time and his willingness to try anything once. The
stoutish dumb-belle, the thinnish blue-belle, and the temperish hair-
belle all come to a country inn and flirt with the young men there,
the stoutish one being pursued by her mother, Mrs. Popham, "an
advanced female" and advocate of women's rights. But when Mrs.
Popham's niece, the prettyish Daisy May, the bicycle re-belle, who
hails from Bradford's own Wellesley and delivers an impassioned
panegyric thereon, arrives, the men all flock to her. Daisy chooses
none of them, and ultimately they return to the other girls. Mrs.
Popham, whose temperance principles do not apply to herself,
matches up with Jorkins, a patent-medicine peddler, who wanders
in and out of the action selling Jorkins's Specific.
    The four later plays require more comment. The earliest was

"Charm" (1907). Hilda Marston has two lovers—Simon Flint, a solid, conscientious, capable, wholly honorable, high-minded businessman, who lacks charm, and Egbert Warren, a fribble, who has it in abundance. The two are cotrustees of her estate. She chooses Egbert, then learns that, to cover his investments in mining stock, he has forged Simon's signature on a note. Though his mother thinks it his duty to both Hilda and the Eternal Verities to send Egbert to prison, Simon covers the note. Hilda, though deeply shocked, refuses to break her engagement, arguing that Egbert now needs her more than ever, and the audience is left feeling that only misery is in store for her.

Hilda is an idealistic, wholly romantic girl, thrilled with the romance of business. Her mother is a fool and Mrs. Flint a stern moralist who plays the game strictly according to the rules. Egbert is a Harold Skimpole–like character; this time Bradford made his beloved Fool-type morally worthless. "Charm" has a vital subject and is well written, though the language is sometimes bookish. The descriptions of the various characters in stage directions show that the author had a very clear conception of them all.

The scene of "Mamma" (1909) is Brookline, Massachusetts, and the play suggests that voting in the state legislature is not always determined by strictly disinterested considerations. Mrs. Windham has a property she wishes the state to buy for an asylum, though the other available site is cheaper and probably more salubriously located. But Mrs. Windham also has a daughter whom, until now, she has always been able to control. Leslie has admirers in the legislature, and her mother is not at all averse to a tieup between the bestowal of her hand and what she regards as the proper vote. Mrs. Windham makes her sale, but, to her astonishment, her daughter does not go along with it. "But I've had my will all my life before."

There is much finagling, involving cross-motives, and there is a large cast of characters, who are handled, on the whole, successfully, for "Mamma" is ingeniously plotted, perhaps even too much so, for the audience might find it difficult to carry all the complications in mind. There is also a butler, who is rather amusing in a

stock way, as he buttonholes everybody he thinks might help him
secure a position in the asylum, where he could make use of his
psychic force, which he believes wasted in his present situation.

Since *Unmade in Heaven* (written in 1909, published in 1917)
is Bradford's only published play, it is naturally the best known.
Though not free of faults, it is also one of the best, partly because
of its unusual, powerful theme and partly because, for once, the
author has avoided unnecessary complications and concentrated
completely upon a single problem. A devout Catholic girl labors
earnestly to convert her Protestant lover and succeeds to such an
extent that he ends by becoming not only a Catholic but also a
priest.

"Unmade in Heaven" was not written as an argument for or against
the Roman Catholic faith. The subject simply presented itself to me as
one of great human and dramatic significance and capable of powerful
theatrical treatment. . . . It is true that the average Protestant American
playgoer has not much interest in the monastic life nor in the priestly
vocation. The idea of certainly breaking a girl's heart for the sake of
doubtfully benefitting humanity through the Church will offend most
Protestant girls as well as Protestant men. They may be offended, but I
do not see how they can fail to be interested, if the problem is presented
in the shape of actual flesh and blood.[2]

It is clear that the author fully appreciates the beauty of the
spiritual ideal and admires those who are capable of devoting their
lives to it. It is also clear that he understands the Catholic approach
to both religious and human problems. Both Eleanor and her lover
Francis are presented with sympathy. Yet they are hardly more than
lay figures or the embodiments of an aspiration or an ideal, and
though the action of the whole play revolves about them, they
are given very little to do; indeed Francis is off stage much of the
time. On the other hand, Eleanor's cousin, Ned Wilde, who loves
her, quite hopelessly and unselfishly, and who is probably Bradford's most attractive Fool, is also a completely humane and attractive representation of human worldliness at its best. Ned is permitted to beard both the high-minded, somewhat fanatical Francis

and the family priest, in the name of the simple humanity which he sees as being outraged and trampled upon, and his obvious kindness and disinterestedness make him difficult to resist.

This leaves only "Who Pays?" (1911). Here, as in "Charm," we have the sensitive girl, this time an aspiring musician, with two suitors—the solid, noble businessman and the flashy pleasure-lover, who is also a musician of considerable talent. And again there is a forgery, generously covered by the businessman, but this time the forgery is committed not by the flashy lover but by the girl's father and has been occasioned by his wife's extravagance. The death blow to the suitor's hopes comes from the revelation that he has a wife living, but this does not add much to his repulsiveness, for he had supposed her dead, and she turns out to be impossibly coarse and vulgar in her single, quite unconvincingly theatrical appearance toward the close of the play. "Who Pays?" is more ambitious than "Charm," with which it obviously has an affinity, with a larger cast of characters and more varied action, and the dialogue is lifelike, though not always greatly varied in style from one character to another. It ends on a strong note of reconciliation, with everybody forgiving everybody, except for the flashy suitor, who disappears; even Madeline's parents, who have lived unhappily for many years, now seem to be turning toward each other with new understanding.

Bradford as Playwright

"I see more and more," wrote Bradford in 1927, "that my plays are all skeletons. They need the flesh of richer observation and more varied color, and above all again, just that same quality of style that makes Sophocles and Shakespeare, and without which the gates of Parnassus will never be opened to us."[3] But the stage door, if not Parnassus, has certainly opened to many who were neither Shakespeare nor Sophocles, and all in all, Bradford's plays are probably about as good as we could expect to have written by an intelligent man and a gifted writer with no practical theatrical experience. He understood his characters, and he knew how to develop a theme, but his action is often stiff and a little awkward (even in *Unmade in Heaven* he does not always manage his "curtains" well), and the analytical note is often overplayed. Except when he was president of the Playgoers Club, he never even had any contacts with theater people; then he got an evening behind the scenes, "on the strict promise on my part that I should not 'monkey with the ballet girls.' Fancy me monkeying with the ballet girls! I should have been more afraid of them than of a collection of wild tigers."[4] Yet the dream "of having one of my comedies acted to a crowded house, of being called before the curtain and making the speech that I have made to myself so many times that I know it better than the Apostles' Creed"[5] never died, and when he participated in a reading of *Unmade in Heaven* in his house, almost at the end of his life, "I had all I could do to restrain my sobs."[6] That same year, he was greatly excited when a woman in Seattle expressed interest in achieving a production and "immediately began to imagine a great triumph for Unmade in Heaven on Broadway and all over the country. Incredible child!"[7]

Chapter Four

Fiction

Bradford wrote nine novels, of which four—*The Private Tutor, Between Two Masters, Matthew Porter,* and *Her Only Way*—were published. There are also a novelette, "Bags of Gold," and a few short stories—"The Photograph," conjecturally assigned to the 1890s, and "Death's Dainty Ways" and "The Meteor," both written in 1920.

The First Two Novels

"Girard" is first mentioned in Bradford's "Journal" on November 22, 1883, and was apparently written in 1884–85. When the author went back to it in 1916, he was surprised by its "literary excellence," finding "the passionate parts written with imagination and rhythmic beauty," and was also pleased with "the general human observation and the variety of characters."[1] So far as the actual writing is concerned, this verdict is just.

Girard, youngest son of the Reverend Elias Cordovan Blake, is an intelligent loner who lives in books and nature and has difficulty establishing communication with his family. He is devoted to Plutarch, Bacon, and Montaigne, has built an altar to Pan in the forest, and prefers Greece and *The Arabian Nights* to anything medieval. Theology fascinates but bewilders him. He has been deeply moved by Emerson and feels least religious in church. His apostasy is deeply felt by his sister Helen, who confides her sorrows to her journal.

Girard turns first to his friend Victoria Gray but finds himself drawn increasingly toward the sensitive and tubercular Mary Clifford, daughter of a clergyman more liberal than Mr. Blake, and the aged Agathon, who had been born in Thessaly and lived through the Greek rebellion against the Turks. Agathon was at one time a Lucretian or Epicurean skeptic, and then a disciple of Leopardi, but he has freed himself from Leopardi's "dark hopeless despair" and now admies Obermann and lives the life of a solitary contemplative. Both Agathon and Mary die, Victoria mates with Mary's brother Henry, and Girard drowns himself, feeling that there is nothing to be gained by continuing to live and that he is going to Mary and into the life of God.

The basic idea for "Girard" came from George Sand's *Lélia*, but the hero was obviously a self-study, and Mary was suggested by Eugénie de Guèrin and Helen Ford, whom Bradford later married and who wrote Mary's journal.[2] The novel is a belated document of the Romantic Movement, closer in spirit to Goethe's *Die Leiden des jungen Werthers*—by which Bradford was fascinated, though he judged the hero weak of will—and other expressions of Continental Romanticism than to their English or American counterparts. It is full of descriptions of natural beauty and literary references (including quotations in foreign languages) and has many soliloquies in the spirit of lyric poetry. Mary's journal and Agathon's papers interrupt the flow of the narrative, and moods and ideas are always more important than story. All in all, "Girard" is the work of a sensitive, talented, highly cultivated young man, who is amazingly erudite for his age but not yet a novelist.

If the second offering, "The Reverend Arthur Meade," written in 1887–89, is not yet a successful novel, it is at least an attempt to write one. The book has an affinity with such other novels of the fin-de-siècle years as Mrs. Humphry Ward's *Robert Elsmere* and Harold Frederic's *The Damnation of Theron Ware* (neither of which had been published when Bradford began his work), for Meade is another young clergyman who loses his faith under the influence of nineteenth-century scientific rationalism. The scene is Arrowside, a village of 700 near Boston, and the story opens with

Meade's installation as pastor of the Congregational church. Here again is a bookish youth, with no experience of life; he finds it impossible to make vital contact with his parishioners and soon realizes that his religion had never been more than intellectual and moral. Both the freethinking Dr. Kay, a comparatively undeveloped character, and the wealthy, worldly Margaret Soule, widowed at twenty-five after a loveless marriage and now ripe for love, complicate his problem. Margaret was suggested by Sallie Ames, later the mother of Van Wyck Brooks, whom Bradford had thought himself in love with for a few weeks, when he was sixteen and she four or five years older.[3] Meade's easygoing clerical neighbor, Larnard, who is greatly at ease in Zion, gives him sympathy, but is too superficial to help him much. Ultimately he resigns his pulpit and leaves town. "I have no faith, no sympathy, no enthusiasm. I am by nature skeptical, critical, profoundly Epicurean." The congregation is moved by his frank confession in his farewell address.

The main line of the plot is simple and uneventful. Meade struggles with his doubts and is finally rejected by Margaret, who turns to Dr. Kay. There are several minor love entanglements and a number of portraits of New England village types. Discussions of music, literature, and travel contribute to the total effect.

The story is told by the omniscient author with many essay-like comments and addresses to the reader. Though Bradford is capable of *showing* how his characters function, he sometimes *tells* us instead, but the scene describing the elaborate party Margaret gives for her simple Arrowside neighbors is well managed.

One of the most interesting things in the book is Bradford's portrayal of the grandeur and nobility of old Deacon Strong, who is estranged from Meade by the latter's liberalism and skepticism, an interesting testimonial to the author's lifelong sympathy with an orthodoxy he could not share. But the Deacon is unconvincing in the scenes where he tries to talk like an Old Testament prophet, not only in rebuking Meade but also in his attack upon his own son for having attended a dance; this kind of thing would have been better accommodated in an Elizabethan play than a novel of New England village life. Margaret, too, is unconvincing at last, not because she rejects Meade, but because, in doing it, she is made to talk like the conventional vampire woman that Bradford had so far successfully avoided making her.

Publication, and After

The Private Tutor, which the author wished to call "A Tutored Savage," was the first novel he managed to get published, by Houghton, Mifflin in 1904; it sold 1,400 copies and went into a second printing. The publisher's title was better than his, for Gordon, not the savage who is never really tutored, is the leading character. The action begins in the Colosseum and partakes in some aspects of the character of a Roman travelogue. Dedicated "To H.F.B. in memory of the weary fascination of Rome," the book obviously derives materials from Bradford's sojourn abroad with his young wife, early in their married life. The epigraph on the title page reads:

> A blossom twinkling from a ruined wall:
> Old stones, young love, and sunshine over all.

The book, however, is not so romantic as that. Gordon is in Europe in charge of Edgar Payne, a young oaf so gauche and brutal that the reader feels a great desire to take him out and step on him, whom his millionaire father wishes to have married to Priscilla Stanton. Priscilla, however, is much too refined to attract him; he gravitates instead to the Countess Markovski, survivor of an affair with Gordon and others, some of whom did not survive; here, if anywhere, *is* Bradford's vampire woman. Priscilla finds her destiny in Gordon, and the Countess sets her cap for Edgar, only to find in the end that, even with all his money, he is more than she can stomach.

The omniscient author is as intrusive in *The Private Tutor* as in "Arthur Meade," and many comments suggest the essayist rather than the novelist; in fact Chapter 3 actually begins: "A friend of mine, whose son had married a young woman from Porto Rico, consoled himself with the remark. . . ." There is a comparatively long passage on the names of cities and another, this time in dialogue, on the merits and demerits of Michelangelo in comparison with other artists and musicians.[4]

Many of the characters are likable and, in the main, believable, though there are scenes which fail to carry conviction. There may be ground for difference of opinion as to whether Edgar is a convincing character, but surely nobody can believe in the Countess in Chapter 21, where she offers to help Gordon with Priscilla if he will help her with Edgar, nor yet in Priscilla's ability to straighten everything out so archly and efficiently as she does in Chapter 26. As has elsewhere been noted, Bradford had already used the story in the play "A Roman Holiday," where the Countess had been allowed to capture Edgar, surely an adequate punishment for the sins of both.

"Autumn Love," which dates from 1904–1905 and opens in "the little ruined theatre at Fiesole, on a bright October afternoon, not many years ago," is certainly Bradford's best unpublished novel; it is difficult to see why it never found a publisher.

In the first chapter, Walter Locke, a twenty-six-year-old novelist, proposes to Virginia Lawrence, thirty-seven, whom he regards as his muse. She refuses him, and he leaves for Rome at once.

Virginia, in Florence, soon realizes that she would have accepted him if she had followed her inclinations. She is visited by George Salisbury, forty, a professor of comparative literature in Nebraska, and by Maurice Lamont, thirty, who, as "Observer," writes moral letters for the *Boston Weekly Preacher* and, as "The Man of the World," frivolous, worldly ones for the *New York Cosmopolite.* He is currently being pursued by Felicia Potts, forty-five, the rich widow of a western miner. Virginia tells him that Miriam Crossman, whom he has loved, is living and painting in Florence, and Maurice renews his proposal to her; Miriam in turn admits that she loves him but declares that she loves her art and independence more.

Still missing Walter, Virginia is joined by her cousin, Lois Carey, twenty, to whom Salisbury is strongly attracted at a dinner Virginia gives for all the principals. The good-hearted Mrs. Potts is adopted into the circle despite her vulgarity, and Miriam undertakes to teach Lois painting.

Walter arrives in the midst of Virginia's Christmas party and announces that he is returning to America to write a novel about modern life, which Virginia, who dislikes realism in literature, opposes. But Lois agrees with him, and Virginia weeps upon being left alone.

Miriam accepts Maurice, then changes her mind, telling him that she loves him but that he is incapable of loving anybody except himself. Lois tells Salisbury that she considers discrepancy in age a barrier to marriage. Walter describes to Lois his idea of writing a novel, "The Prophet of Joy," whose theme is essentially that of the narrative poem Bradford himself would publish in 1920. Maurice finally yields to Mrs. Potts, and Miriam gives a party to celebrate their engagement. Lois being at home with a cold, Virginia brings the situation to a head by sending Walter to her, while she herself accepts Salisbury, and only Miriam is left unmated.

The plot of "Autumn Love" is not superior to that of *The Private Tutor*, but the general effect is more impressive. If Maurice's surrender to Mrs. Potts is hurried and not wholly convincing, there is only one incredible scene, in Chapter 15, where, before having made up his mind, he pretends to make love to her in an art gallery, but this is passed over quickly. Both the Italian landscape and the art objects in Italian galleries are brought into the story with some skill, and there is considerable commentary on Botticelli and Rubens and Michelangelo's *David*, in the manner to which the world became accustomed in *Romola* and *The Marble Faun*. Maurice is obviously the character who is closest to the author. At one point he tells Salisbury that his gaiety is a skeleton under flowers: "Life, to me, is so intensely serious, so horribly tragic, that I don't see how those who take it seriously endure it at all."

More Success and Failure

Between Two Masters (1906), which Houghton, Mifflin insisted upon calling the book Bradford had written in 1905 as "God and

Mammon," was a much more serious and ambitious novel than its predecessors. Amos Phelps, a rich banker and broker, nearing the end of his life, intends his business and his athletic stepdaughter Ethel for his nephew Harvey Phelps, who is just out of Harvard; but Harvey, who is under the influence of a saintly friend, the Reverend Marcus Upham, has his doubts about the capitalistic system and cares less for Ethel than for her schoolteacher friend Milly Erskine. When the firm's manipulations in copper lead to the suicide of one of his acquaintances, Harvey withdraws from State Street, and, having taken counsel of Upham, spends the summer working with a boys' club at Robertsville.

Through an accidental and innocent involvement in another tragedy, touching a humble Irish family, the O'Briens, Harvey meets a high-minded settlement worker, Diana Newton, and becomes interested in settlement work. Mr. Phelps dies, and Harvey gets deeper into public-service work and introduces Diana to Marcus, now the pastor of a small church near Boston, who falls in love with her and is further spiritualized by his failure to win her. Ethel accepts the journalist George Kent, and Harvey is begged by her to come into the firm and by Milly, in effect, to marry her. He declines both propositions, feeling that his way of life is at last beginning to grow clear to him. In the end he gets Diana and becomes head of the settlement.

Though *Between Two Masters* performed less successfully in the book stores than *The Private Tutor*, it is a far more significant novel. Nowhere did Bradford show himself more aware of the injustices in our social structure, and nowhere else did he come as close to the solution of life's problems through religion. At the end, Harvey

shook the fetters of the world's servitude forever from his limbs. . . . The bonds were burst, the walls were faded, the bars were shattered. The life in God, the love of God seemed not to be a giving but an immense acquiring of light, of power, and of joy, something to be held, something positive, to be imparted to others, to be spread broadcast, as far as one's influence would reach. Overhead, beyond the moon and stars, is love, everywhere love. And underneath are the everlasting arms.[5]

In one of his confidences to the reader of the undated novel, "The Crackling of Thorns," Bradford fears that he may have too many heroines and that no one of them is very heroic; "in fact some of them are a little vulgar." The "genuine heroine" is Ada Gilbert, youngest daughter of a wealthy barbarian who lives on Boston's Commonwealth Avenue, and Vina Macelroy, his stenographer, who lives on Columbus Avenue and intrigues to marry him, is the "false one." Bradford based Ada on Vida D. Scudder, as he imagined she might have been in her youth.[6] But there is vulgarity in Gilbert's older daughters and their admirers, too, except for Bob Gardiner, "an honest, clean-minded American boy," who shows his good taste by his attraction to Ada. The girl's own humanity and sensitivity to social issues appear when she persuades her father to give Peters, who has been discharged for drinking, a second chance and his employees a half-holiday with a picnic at his place in the country. But Peters gets drunk again and turns nasty, so that there is nothing for it but to have Bob toss him at last into the pond, and Gilbert's employees, who resent being patronized, find more exciting adventures on their afternoon off than have been formally provided for them.

"The Secret of Woodbine Lodge," sometimes called "Madam Mystery," which is dated 1908 in the Houghton index, is not, despite its title, a detective story. There is no crime, and the "secret" is a very mild one, for Aurelia Bell, whose sojourn at Woodbine Lodge puts Deerford aflutter, is only sitting out the time until her trustee, the explorer Sterling Hayden, shall return from an expedition and she can make up her mind whether she wishes to marry him, and the reader learns all this almost at the beginning. To be sure, it is also revealed at the end that she is the daughter of Senator Stollprecht by an early marriage to a chorus girl, but very little is made of this, and it contributes nothing to the interest.

The story is fairly well managed, and there are many scenes of social gatherings, which embrace some undeveloped characters, with an abundance of good talk, which does little to advance the action. Dr. Barrows, himself an aspiring explorer, who is not quite sure whether he is more attracted to Aurelia or to her money, and who gets it into his head that she is a blackmailer and political agent and threatens to expose her unless she will give him what he wants, is really more jackass than villain. A more attractive character is the church organist, Richards, an aspiring composer, who is also attracted to Aurelia, but whose true love is Edith Winter, with whom he is united at the end of the book. Another minor love affair between Evelyn Hilliard and Dick Steele, who has already been rejected by Aurelia, peters out when Evelyn decides that she does not wish to be tied down, at least until after she has made her own way. Obviously Bradford's long immersion in the Elizabethan drama must have been responsible for his addiction to the abundance of romantic subplots in both his novels and his plays. The Elizabethan note is sounded again here in the presence of the Fool George Buckingham ("Flitters"), who has much more to do in *Matthew Porter* than in this book, where he does not accomplish very much, and in the highly theatrical and somewhat hurried and abrupt scene at the close, where Dr. Barrows is refused once more at Aurelia's last party, and is about to "expose" her when he is cut off by Hayden's return and Aurelia's announcement of her engagement to him.

Matthew Porter and the Rest

Matthew Porter (1908), which Bradford had wished to call "God Save the Commonwealth," was the last novel he managed to get published in book form. It is not without its faults. The development is somewhat stiff and formal, largely in terms of set "scenes," and there are some incredible confrontations. The book is overcrowded, too; there are parties, a musical, a picnic, a masquerade, a debate in Faneuil Hall, and a convention; no one of these scenes is badly managed, but there are too many such events. The "bad" heroine, Margaret Ferguson, who marries Porter's rival Dudley Heath, whom she does not love, apparently to spite him, Porter, and herself, is hardly a believable character, and some readers may

feel that Porter himself is too much idealized and that the development, not only moral but intellectual, of the "good" heroine, Viola
Buckingham, who enters the book as the toplofty sybil of a very
superior salon and goes out as a passionate champion of political
idealism and the common weal, fails to carry complete conviction.
Nevertheless the book has scope as well as a high aim and an important theme, and some allowance must be made for the demands
of a *Tendenzroman* whose primary purpose was to dramatize the
convictions concerning the reform and revitalization of state government whose advocacy had been the main life purpose of the author's
father, to whom the book was dedicated.

With the Republican machine controlling Massachusetts state
politics, Matthew Porter offers himself for governor on the Democratic ticket. Porter's basic idea is "to shake up the legislature and
put it into its place—let the governor do the governing" and "have
a cabinet," which would "put the secretaries right into the legislature, as in England," not so that all the legislation might originate
with him but to ensure "free and open legislative discussion, in
which the executive, as representing the whole state, should have
a leading part."[7] Porter and Dudley Heath, who is merely a pawn
in the hands of his uncle, William J. Wood, the corrupt Republican
boss, are rivals for the hand of Margaret Ferguson, who will accept
Porter only if he agrees to give up politics and accept the offer of
her father, the traffic magnate Nathan Ferguson, to enter business.
Hinckley, chairman of the Democratic state committee, works
against Porter behind the scenes, even to the extent of accepting
$20,000 from Wood to help in Porter's defeat. But Porter wins the
labor boss Smith and the editor Wingate and is triumphantly elected
in the last chapter.

Through her cousin George Buckingham ("Flitters"), the Republicans introduce Porter to the salon of Viola Buckingham, hoping
that she will be a Delilah to him. He does fall in love with her, as
they had hoped; what they had not counted on was that she should
also fall in love not only with him but with his cause and develop
besides into a masterly writer of campaign documents which contribute importantly to his victory. The net result of their intrigue

therefore is that they have helped Porter to win not only the governorship but a devoted wife.

Her Own Way is dated 1910 at Houghton, but though Robert Frost made a valiant attempt to get Henry Holt and Company to publish it, it did not appear in print until 1924, when it ran through four numbers of *The Stratford Monthly*. There is an abundance of dialogue in this novel, and Bradford was proud of it. The characters are again Americans abroad, this time in Antwerp and Lucerne, near the end of the nineteenth century, and the subject matter is wooing and mating.

Mrs. Hart does not wish her son Philip to remain unmarried; she merely wishes him to marry the girl she has chosen for him, Jeannette Munroe. Philip, however, falls in love with Florence Caswell, the daughter of an easygoing retired Unitarian clergyman, a rather charming character. When Philip first proposes to Florence, she refuses him, telling him he is a child without purpose in life; later she admits she loves him but sends him away for a month. When he follows her to Lucerne, they come to an understanding, and Jeannette is thoughtfully provided for by Mrs. Hart's nephew, Gilbert Warren, who is writing a book on Gothic architecture which he does not seem anxious to finish.

Since there is nothing in *Her Own Way* to grip the reader very deeply, Bradford was right in basing the claim of the story upon its dialogue, which is graceful and lively. Florence waxes oddly and uncharacteristically sentimental in Chapter 30, where she is sure she will learn to love Mrs. Hart, but the scene in Chapter 32, in which Philip and his mother make their peace with each other, is rather touching. Another excellent scene is that in Chapter 24, in which Florence, having been remonstrated with by Mrs. Hart, tells her frankly that she will decide whether or not to accept her son, not on the basis of whether it would please Jeannette or his mother, but solely with reference to the needs and desires of the persons immediately concerned. Did Bradford have in mind here Elizabeth Bennet's famous interview with Lady Catherine de Bourgh in *Pride and Prejudice*? His own scene would be no unworthy descendant.

Bradford was obviously not greatly interested in his short stories, and nothing needs to be said of the three completed specimens mentioned at the beginning of this chapter but that they are all ironical and make use of a surprise ending.[8] His only novelette, "Bags of Gold," which was written for *Ainslee's* in 1908 but declined, is of more interest, for here we find him attempting the mystery story from which he had rather oddly shied in "The Secret of Woodbine Lodge." The bags of gold found by plumbers while working in Mrs. Barlow's house disappear overnight, like Wilkie Collins's Moonstone. Through the skillful detective work of Walter Young, it is shown that Enid's unworthy lover, Gilbert Lynde, was involved in the robbery. There are just enough complicating elements to mislead the reader and keep him in suspense but not too many to be handled comfortable in fifty-six pages. Naturally Walter gets the girl.

The Novels in General

Since the novel is a far more flexible form than the drama, Bradford had less difficulty here in getting his characters on and off, but still with a tendency to stiffness and overreliance for development on one arranged confrontation after another. The author's weakness for subplots led him to use a larger number of characters than he needed or had time and space to develop, and if his people sometimes seem to understand themselves and each other more completely than we do in life, the reason probably is that his mind was essentially that of a critic or essayist rather than, in the narrower sense of the term, a creative writer. His dialogue is often excellent, and if his subject matter sometimes seems trifling, we must remember his rooted conviction that humor and lightness of tone were the qualities in which contemporary fiction was most deficient.

In 1920 he thought he liked "Autumn Love" and "Woodbine Lodge" best among his novels; two years later, he rated *Matthew Porter* a great book. He could sell himself short, as when he wrote Lyman Beecher Stowe, then associated with Doubleday, that his novels were quaint, old-fashioned things, depending on ease and naturalness of dialogue and character-study, and with altogether too little story interest. Especially are they entirely out of the current style: no adultery in them, no sordidness, no Main Street or Babbitt detail whatever, just pleasant people doing and saying pleasant things, after the much-despised Victorian way, with the author trying to lift a little bit of the veil that always shrouds our souls.[9]

Sometimes, too, he thought his novels failures because he had not had sufficiently wide contacts with life. But probably his most considered comment was the one he addressed to himself and ended with a question:

I have such a wonderful gift of words, and I have such power of constructing, of putting things together with symmetry and adaptation and emphasis and climax, and I have such knowledge of human nature, and above all I have, what counts more for intelligent readers in a novel than anything else, the gift of brilliant and telling and natural dialogue. Why cannot I write novels? Why? Why? Why, My God, why?[10]

Chapter Five

Psychography in General

Definitions and Influences

The general reader knows Gamaliel Bradford almost exclusively as the inventor and leading exponent of psychography. A psychograph is a picture of the soul or the psyche, a study of the character and personality of a human being. Bradford coined the word for himself and then discovered that George Saintsbury had already used it to describe the work of Charles Augustin Sainte-Beuve (1804–1869). Though it indicates accurately what the character writers try to do, the uninitiated are always in danger of supposing that it must have an affinity with psychoanalysis or some kind of psychological vagary. This troubled Bradford sufficiently that by 1924 he had stopped pushing the word. Unfortunately there is no really satisfactory substitute.

The most widely used term to indicate a piece of biographical writing which emphasizes character rather than events is "portrait," and for convenience this term will sometimes be employed in these pages. Yet Bradford himself often expounded its inadequacy, never more effectively than in the Preface to *Union Portraits*:

The portrait-painter presents his subject at a particular moment of existence, with full and complete individuality of that moment, but with only the most indirect suggestion of all the varied and complicated stages of life and character that have preceded. The object of the psychographer is precisely the opposite. From the complex of fleeting experiences that make up the total of man's or woman's life he endeavors

72

to extricate those permanent habits of thought and action which constitute what we call character, and which, if not unchangeable, are usually modified only by a slow and gradual process. His aim further is to arrange and treat these habits or qualities in such a way as to emphasize their relative importance, and to illustrate them by such deeds and words, as, irrespective of chronological sequence, shall be most significant and most impressive.[1]

In later years, he often used the word "souls," "in sheer desperation, because portraits was so utterly unsatisfactory and psychographs is still pedantic. But souls is abominably pretentious and I suspect has destroyed my reputation with the learned and scholarly everywhere."[2] Actually "souls" is less pretentious than vague, and it has religious associations which are here out of place.

What, then, is the difference between psychography and biography as commonly conceived? A biography tells the story of a man's life; a psychograph probes his character and personality. A biographer arranges his materials chronologically, a psychographer topically.

As for formal psychology, Bradford saw it as the antithesis of all biography. "Biography is the study of the individual, pursued with all the aids of psychology, but always centered on the individual at last. Psychology is constantly and properly occupied with the general and uses the individual only to illustrate its general laws and conclusions."[3] In Freud he found only "a distortion and exaggeration and fantastic elaboration and misunderstanding of perfectly plain and long known facts."[4] But he got nothing from Roback or MacDougall either, or, in a different area, from such a writer as Spengler. "I was brought up in a storm of general principles. My father lived with them, delighted in them, and talked about them perpetually. He was quick and keen to note facts, but every fact instantly became the text for some large, sweeping deduction and assertion."[5] Since the son had tied himself to reality by concentrating on the individual, he could hardly have been expected to be pleased when the psychologists threatened to take biography over.

Bradford was not of course the first biographical writer to con-

cern himself with the analysis of character. He knew Plutarch (after
whom he named one of his cats) and those famous passages which
compare eminent Greeks and Romans. He mentions Tacitus, Clarendon, Saint-Simon, as well as Matthew Arnold's essay on Falkland
and Lowell's on "A Great Public Character," and he must also have
been familiar with the biographical writings of Dr. Johnson, Macaulay, Carlyle, Thackeray, Stevenson, and others.

But it was such French writers as Scherer, Boissier, Lemaître,
and, best of all, Sainte-Beuve that Bradford regarded as his masters.
The strange thing about Sainte-Beuve is that he treated between
seven and eight hundred individuals without ever realizing that he
was a psychographer at all. He never detached psychography from
literary criticism (most of his work was occasioned by recent publications and appeared first in newspapers) and never developed a
method. As Bradford put it to William Roscoe Thayer:

It was a complete mistake for him to regard himself as a literary critic.
Such work as the portraits of women in volume II of the *Lundis*, the
finest things he ever did, are no more literary criticism than your *Cavour*
or *Hay*. His admirable characterization of himself as "a naturalist of
souls" has nothing whatever to do with literary criticism. . . . In practically all his portraits and articles, he pursues the purely chronological
method of biography, narrating the matter of the study in its historical
sequence and grafting comment and emphasis upon it as he goes along.
I have parted from this process altogether, whether wisely or not only
experience can show, but in any case with deliberate purpose.[6]

Sainte-Beuve generally begins with a generalization, sometimes
original, sometimes quoted. The first sentence of the Mary Stuart
is from Scott. The first paragraph of the Cowper contains a brief
bibliography. He moves up to his subject gradually, and the line of
approach may be historical, philosophical, or personal. In the Madame de Sévigné he takes us through a lengthy description of the
literary and social characteristics of the subject's time; in the Madame de Krudener he speculates first on what she might have been
like had she lived in a different period. The third section of the
Cowper is almost entirely criticism: analysis of the quality of

Cowper's poetry, ecstatic praise of the simple life reflected in it, a discussion of the poet's place in literature, and a comparison between him and the author of *Paul et Virginie*. When Sainte-Beuve deals with a comparatively unfamiliar writer, he is even capable of giving detailed synopses of works. Moralizing seduces him always, and when writing of contemporaries he may be misled by personal emotions. Indeed, though he did gain in objectivity during later years, many passages can only be called autobiographical.

He is very likely to use long quotations—whole poems or letters —only a small portion of which he needs to make his point. Some sections in his discussions of poets look more like anthologies than either biography or criticism. He never learned the art of employing only brief, relevant quotations and building them into his text. What Bradford owed to him was inspiration; his method was his own.

Comparisons and Contrasts

In the 1920s Bradford shared his fame as a biographical writer with such contemporaries as Lytton Strachey, André Maurois, and Emil Ludwig. H. L. Mencken "boomed" Bradford as "the man who invented the formula of Strachey's *Eminent Victorians*," and because Strachey was riding high at the time and Mencken's name was believed capable of selling books, Bradford's publishers emblazoned this statement over his jackets for years; he himself, though grateful for Mencken's interest, was quite aware that it represented only a journalistic simplification. The one thing for which Mencken deserves credit is that he did realize that Bradford had been first in the field and that he was not imitating Strachey, as some others had been ignorant enough to believe. But Strachey, Maurois, Ludwig, and the others all wrote straightforward chronological biography; if they were "new" biographers, it was in spirit, not method.

Bradford would not have been human if it had not stung him to realize that Strachey was much more popular than he. For some time he refused to read him, but when he did he capitulated completely and became an admirer. There was some correspondence, warm and friendly, though not intimate, they exchanged books, and Bradford dedicated *Daughters of Eve* "To Lytton Strachey, who makes biography not only a curious science but an exquisite art." He even went so far as to write the Englishman that the chief difference between them was not method but genius. Both were interested in "the quick, intense delineation of souls," but Strachey did it "by the direct natural method," while Bradford's own was "too static; yours is dynamic; gives your personages a strange and clinging vitality which I am always in danger of losing."[7] Nevertheless he was well aware that he had some qualities Strachey lacked, and he was never in danger of abandoning psychography to imitate anybody and slip back into the biographical main stream.

Bradford did fear, however, that in dealing topically with the qualities of character which, in varying guises, appear in all men, psychography might become repetitive and monotonous, and he feared that in dealing, as it must, with more or less permanent traits, it might allow insufficiently for changes and developments. Unlike the portrait painter, who must confine himself to what he can see at a particular time, the psychographer *can* take account of such things; by the same token, the chronological biographer *can* describe character. But the biographer deals with character only as it manifests itself in connection with particular actions which may be widely separated in time, and the psychographer does tend toward generalization, however carefully his generalizations may be supported by reference to particular actions or utterances. Other things being equal, the biography is, then, best adapted to showing what the man *did*, the psychograph to what he *was*, and since most readers care more for narrative than exposition and are more interested in story than in character, biography will probably always be more popular than psychography. Two of Bradford's special admirers, Ambrose White Vernon and Richard C. Cabot, were particularly concerned about the difficulty of indicating developments in psychographs, and Bradford did his best to give due weight to their objections. Essentially, however, he agreed with Sainte-Beuve that "the larger traits of character are fixed and remain so, from the cradle to the grave. We are constantly misled as to developments by the appearance of permanent traits in new manifestations, owing to the endless play of circumstance. But the traits are there, from the beginning."[8]

Bradford had no desire to play Rhadamanthus and little interest in biography as "either commemoration or example." He wished to depict human beings as they were under the influence of "the universal and pervading influence of the scientific spirit," but since the values of science and art are never quite the same, we may perceive that he has a divided mind about this when he adds that "the artistic side of biography" is what interests him most.[9] He once wrote that he regarded his subjects "infinitely more from the point of scientific curiosity than either approval or disapproval,"[10] but since scientific detachment and lack of sympathy are precisely what he criticizes in Sainte-Beuve, it is not surprising that he should also have worried about the moral influence of his work: if, as he says, Darwinism had wrecked the moral and religious universe for him, he did not wish to have even a small share in wrecking it for others.

Working Methods, Style, and Technique

Bradford's ideal was to build his psychographs into a tight structure in which one topic led to another in order of climax so that the character emerged at last in terms of an almost organic unity. Structure and the use of quotations were the two aspects of his work to which he gave the most careful attention, using quotations both as evidence, to support his own observations, deductions, and generalizations, and for atmosphere, to bring the reader, as it were, into the subject's presence and allow him to hear his voice. Unlike Sainte-Beuve's, his quotations are characteristically short and woven into his text.

In an early letter, he went so far as to describe his portraits as consisting "largely of carefully selected brief quotations from the person's own words, woven together so as to give as complete and rounded a portrayal of him as possible."[11] But this was an exaggeration even then, and it became more an exaggeration as time marched on. When he wrote of the politicos treated in *As God Made Them* and *The Quick and the Dead*, he found himself quoting much less than of old. "I come more and more to sum up and condense the results of my own thought and study and depend less and less upon the actual words of the subject for illustration." This was partly because his subjects were now somewhat less eloquent or quotable than the more imaginative figures with whom he had concerned himself in, say, *Bare Souls*, but he also thought that his work on the religious trilogy had encouraged his tendency toward generalization.[12]

Not all Bradford's quotations are from his subject, however, nor yet from what others have written about him. His wide reading nowhere stood him in better stead than when it brought to mind quotations from recondite sources which could not have been researched for the subject under consideration yet which illuminate and not infrequently dignify it significantly. Many of these are naturally from Shakespeare, who can be depended upon, sooner or later, to say something about everything, as when Dolly Madison's equability brings the banished Duke of *As You Like It* to mind:

> Happy is your grace
> That can translate the stubbornness of fortune
> Into so quiet and so sweet a style.

But *The Maid's Tragedy* of Beaumont and Fletcher suits quite as well to indicate the nature of what both Mrs. Longstreet and Mrs. Jefferson wrote of their husbands:

> Those have most power to hurt us that we love:
> We lay our sleeping lives within their arms.[13]

Who but Bradford would have turned to *The Imitation of Christ* in connection with the domestic bickering of Mr. and Mrs. Samuel Pepys—"After winter comes summer, after night the day, and after a storm a sweet calm"—and who else would have closed a study of Ninon de Lenclos with quotations from Matthew Arnold and

Sophocles or compared Madame de Maintenon with Benjamin Franklin, Julie de Lespinasse with Sarah Butler, or Catherine the Great with Aaron Burr?[14]

In preparing his psychographs, Bradford had the unusual habit of leaving the reading of his basic sources until last. There were times when he floundered a bit trying to get hold of his subject; then, suddenly, as with the Clay, perhaps while he lay awake in bed of a morning, "the portrait suddenly took on color and glory," and he proceeded to make his outline and dream up perfectly stunning sentences to close the various sections.[15] When he had some preliminary familiarity with his subject, the whole plan sometimes emerged at an amazingly early stage. He realized that, in following such procedure, he might get his mind frozen into "preconceived views of the character," but he did not change his ways. The one thing he could be sure of was that all the hard work would be done in his head, not at his desk.

I never write a line until I have got my material together. I generally make an elaborate plan at a very early stage, then rather copious notes from all sorts of sources, then when everything is ready, I seat myself at the typewriter and compose my first draft at about a thousand words an hour. The first draft is to all intents and purposes final. . . . All the labor of my work is in the making of the plan, which I do in the minutest detail. When that is in the proper shape, the words come of themselves.[16]

In connection with *Daughters of Eve*, he speaks of each portrait's being

carefully divided into fifteen or twenty sections and for each of these sections is allotted so many pages or half or quarter pages. Then I permit myself to exceed these limits, but only in such fashion as not to destroy or seriously interfere with the original proportions.[17]

When a high-school class had difficulty outlining his portrait of Henry Ford, he described his method in minute detail in a long letter to the teacher and showed how every paragraph fitted into the plan.[18]

Though he was never able to write more than two or three hours a day and was often so sick that he could not write at all, Bradford's production was rapid. He generally planned to give about two months to the reading he did for a psychograph in one of his composite books and about eight days to the writing. Unlike the specialist who stays with a single subject throughout his working lifetime and produces a number of books and articles about him, he moved from subject to subject. In a sense he was more interested in his method than in any particular individual to whom he applied it, but he would have preferred to say that his interest was in the humanity embodied in the individuals with whom he dealt and which he hoped his method would bring out. While he was at work on a book or a portrait, the subject was his whole life. He might believe he preferred creative writing to psychography, he might even believe all writing was torture, but when he got wrapped up in what he was doing, he was in bliss. To be sure, the torture remained. Approaching the end of a portrait, he might be sure that "the large part already done is in every way successful, still until the last stroke is added it seems impossible that I should achieve what I want. And then when it is all done, the nervous reaction of getting through with it is equal to the nervous strain of carrying it on."[19] But when he was through, he was through. People kept sending him Civil War and Lee material as late as when he was working on Moody and Darwin, and he wanted to ask them what the Civil War was and who was Lee. Yet, when he went back to the general in 1931 to do a biographical sketch of him for the high-school book D. C. Heath wanted, his interest quickly revived.

All this often caused Bradford to accuse himself of superficiality. How could a man dare to write about Moody without being a trained scholar in the field of religious studies or about Darwin without being a scientist? He comforted himself with two reflections: he was striving for suggestiveness rather than finality, and he was not giving an account of the man's work as such but merely studying his character and personality as revealed through it and otherwise. Though he knew as well as anybody that nobody could deal definitively with Catherine the Great without having devoted a lifetime of study to her and to Russia, he could still write, with endearing naïveté, "I have at least material to make a brilliant, profound, many sided human portrait,"[20] and it is only fair to add that the experts were often pleased. Frederick L. Paxson praised his Blaine, Aubrey H. Starke called his study of Sidney Lanier the best thing that had been written about the poet, and Colonel House was delighted with the Woodrow Wilson. It seemed to Bradford again that the limited time and space at his disposal necessitated his choosing his materials with the utmost care and thus enabled him to snatch an advantage from the jaws of necessity (he showed the same nervous restlessness in his writing as in his reading by the clock), and the general reader does not know whether to be more impressed by what he did or what he left undone. He went through seven solid volumes of medieval Latin for Thomas à Kempis and seven thousand double-columned pages of French for Fénelon and took about 20,000 words of notes for Henry Ford and for Madame de Maintenon, besides the passages he marked in the books he owned. Yet he produced his psychograph of Voltaire after having read only "a small proportion" of his published writings and "little more than half" of his correspondence, which he was hoarding because he enjoyed it so much that he wanted it to outlast his lifetime,[21] and for all his devotion to Sainte-Beuve he never read all his works.

Though Bradford always feared that his powers might be waning with age, his last books were among his best, and when he died, he had many in mind that he did not live to write. "Getters and Spenders" would have included one of the Fuggers or one of the Genoese bankers, Rothschild, and Astor or Rockefeller under the first category, and Lucullus, Law, Fox or Sheridan, and Hearst under the second. "Frolic Souls" would have embraced Aristophanes, Rabelais, Cervantes, Sterne, and Heine, and "Dreamers and Doers" would have juxtaposed Caesar, Cromwell, and Napoleon against Plato, Rousseau, and Emerson. "Documents of Nature" was to deal with the great letter-writers (one wonders just how it would have dif-

fered from *Bare Souls*), and we might have had the great poets in
"The Book of Secrecy" ("In Nature's infinite book of secrecy/A
little can I read"), as well as "The Book of Thinkers" and something called "Platform and Hearth." "Women of Today," in connection with which he mentions Margot Asquith, Edna Ferber,
Queen Mary (consort of George V), and others would seem to have
been the least promising subject; the most teasing was "Loves and
Hates," in which he planned to deal with persons like Scott and
Jules Lemaître, whom he greatly admired, and with others, like
Carlyle and Mrs. Browning, whom he greatly disliked, treating both
groups with equal fairness.[22]

Bradford used exclamations, rhetorical questions, and addresses
to the reader freely, especially in his earlier work. "Oh, the truth
of history!" "Oh, to have been present at that dinner!" "How I
should like to have heard him!" "Something to love here, is there
not?" "Could you imitate her, madam?" "Remember this, when you
read some of the following extracts and you will wonder as I do."
"God knows, a husband's love is a pitiful thing." Even, "Whew!"[23]
He was also capable of directly expressing his attitude toward a
subject and of open reference to his own experience. Thus he speaks
of Madame de Sévigné as "this beautifully rounded character,"
parts from Seward with the greatest reluctance, thanks heaven that
General Sherman did not talk more, is glad that Stanton did not
write his contemplated book on the Bible (since in this case Bradford would have had to read it), and is so moved by an utterance
of General Thomas that he feels the tears in his eyes. We know that
he was thinking of his father when he wrote of Theodore Roosevelt's perpetual vehemence, "I speak with feeling, having passed a
considerable portion of my life with just such a character," and he
was obviously thinking of himself when he wrote of the health of
Alexander H. Stephens, "How far this fiery energy of the soul was
responsible for the failure of the body, who shall say?"[24]

He could build up to a quotation when he thought it necessary
or interpret its implications after he had presented it. Thus when
Mrs. James G. Blaine calls her husband "the best man I have ever
known," and then adds, "Do not misunderstand me. I do not say

that he is the best man that ever lived, but that of the men I have thoroughly known, he is the best," Bradford adds, "Could the interplay of qualifying analysis and passionate affection be better illustrated than in that? The more one ponders on the sentence, the more one is impressed by the rich significance of it."[25]

His comments on his quotations and observations could be mischievous, as in "I imagine that after six months of marriage, Mrs. Sumner came to have a certain tenderness for the memory of Preston Brooks." They could also be devastating. Mrs. Jefferson Davis says her husband had the gift "for governing men without humiliating them," but Bradford thought she had got it turned completely around. Woodrow Wilson enjoyed the admiration of women. "There is nothing more bewitching than to have an agreeable woman discover that you are a genius—especially when you have already surmised it yourself." Mussolini is not "intoxicated with grandeur" but would "like to be intoxicated with humility." "Perhaps he is; it is so hard not to be intoxicated with something."[26]

Bradford admits that there is much that cannot be known about his subjects, and sometimes he speculates about the unknown—though never without serving notice on the reader that he is speculating. Two passages in the Theodore Roosevelt illustrate the relevant and irrelevant use of anecdote (the latter is very rare in Bradford). After his children had heard Roosevelt tell Mrs. Storer he would rather have one of them die than grow up a weakling, they came to him and reported, "Father, we have consulted as to which of us must die, and we have decided that it shall be the baby." This is merely amusing, but the story of how Roosevelt once startled his wife and John Burroughs by bringing his fist down upon the table, killing a mosquito "with a blow that would almost have demolished an African lion," inspires a comment which sums up one whole aspect of his character: "He killed mosquitoes as if they were lions, and lions as if they were mosquitoes."[27]

When he was criticized for his use of apostrophes and rhetorical questions, Bradford told his journal, "Well, I like them, and if my public does not, it may be damned."[28] He was deeply hurt, however, when Mark Van Doren, reviewing *The Soul of Samuel Pepys*, cruelly spoke of his "fatuous familiarity which grows increasingly offensive,"[29] the more so because he himself feared he had overworked his informality in that particular volume. He told Van Doren and he told himself that the former had rendered him a service and thereafter held himself in greater check.[30]

Ellery Sedgwick liked best those portraits of Bradford's which had some spice or satire in them. Nevertheless his outstanding characteristic as a psychographer was a wide-ranging sympathy and pity; as has already been observed he saw the absence of this element as Sainte-Beuve's greatest limitation. When Dr. W. W. Keen thought he had handled Catherine the Great too gently, he replied, "But it [is] always my principle not indeed to slight the frailties but to make them comparatively unimportant where there are great human qualities beside them."[31] It was characteristic that he should admit the addiction of both Toombs and Hooker to alcohol but treat it only incidentally, yet he is generally pretty scrupulous about noting exceptions to his generalizations about character, even when he plays them down.

Though he could not help liking some of his subjects better than others, Bradford opposed Maurois's view that the biographer should select only persons with whom he felt sympathy.

The truth is he should be in sympathy with all his subjects. For the time he should become the soldier, the saint, the scholar, the artist, the lover, the toiler, even the sinner, not in the fact of his sin, but in the possibility of it. It is by this universal sympathy that he makes his biography real and alive, and he can thus awaken in his readers the sympathy that he feels himself.[32]

In 1930 he expressed the view that "just because I have no character of my own, it sometimes seems to me that I have a lot of other peoples'" and that "though I have no life of my own, I live passionately in the lives of others,"[33] and that same year, characteristically adapting himself to his correspondent, he played down the moral element in his work in a letter to Mencken:

More and more, I am afraid, I get to study all kinds of human beings for the pure interest of them, without the slightest desire to commend or the opposite. I see so much to admire as well as so much to disapprove of in myself, that I am singularly tolerant of the weaknesses and even of the virtues—which sometimes require more tolerance—of other people.[34]

But he was truer to his own temperament and practice when he confided to his journal concerning Moody:

I must try above all to enter into Moody's own state of mind and inner life, to see the world as he sees it and interpret it as he interprets it. But all that time, as always, there is and must be the play of my own spirit above and beyond all this.[35]

In the vast majority of his psychographs, Bradford achieved both these ends. The first achievement made him one of the most perceptive of biographers, and the second explains why, though they read most biographers because they are interested in their subjects, people read Bradford, regardless of this consideration, because they are interested in him.[36]

Chapter Six

The Psychographs, I

The Road to Psychography:
Types of American Character (1895) and
A Naturalist of Souls (1917, 1926)

In 1922 Gamaliel Bradford wrote of his first book, *Types of American Character*, that "it anticipated in an abstract sort of way the kind of work I am doing at present."[1] It is the only book in which he deals with types rather than individuals, and, remembeirng such character-writers of the seventeenth century as Sir Thomas Overbury, John Earle, and Joseph Hall, who were similarly employed, the seasoned reader of English literature might, a priori, be conditioned to look for their influence upon Bradford. He does not mention any of them, however, and the only essay in the volume from which support for the theory of influence might possibly be derived is the last, "The Scholar."

The other titles are, in order, "The American Pessimist," "The American Idealist," "The American Epicurean," "The American Philanthropist," "The American Man of Letters," and "The American Out of Doors." Though all these types are carefully defined, the method of development is historical, the various figures are seen in relationship to their cultural inheritance, and in a number of cases the distinctively American modifications of the types under consideration do not emerge until the development of the essay is well under way. The book is very well written, and its range of references to classical, English, continental, and American literature is extremely wide for so young a writer.

Except for his frequent references to and quotations from Emerson, the author takes a rather dim view of American literature. He inclines to think that both the novel and the drama have had their day, and though he looks hopefully toward the development of a distinctively American humor, he never mentions Mark Twain. But he has freer, more far-ranging references to contemporary American life in many aspects than he often allowed himself in later books. Though he already finds the Puritans unattractive because they lacked idealism and sees Christian morality surviving largely without the dogmatic support which it had enjoyed in the past and the churches largely apologetic, recharactering an ancient faith in contemporary, sometimes irrelevant, terms, he quotes the Bible frequently and gives a general impression of the "right-thinking," forward-looking patriotism characteristic of the time the book appeared. The nineteenth-century faith in "progress" keeps its hold upon him: he does not believe that Americans are corrupt or decadent, and he is, as he never ceased to be, humanitarian.

A Naturalist of Souls is much more relevant to our discussion. Though its publication postdated that of the Civil War books, it is the key document for the study of Bradford's psychography, for it is the only volume in which we see his method in the making. The first studies were planned as straight literary criticism, but as one turns the successive pages, psychography emerges, develops, and at last takes over altogether, the pivotal chapter being the one on Clarendon, analyzing "the work and the character of one to whom psychography is deeply indebted for models and inspiration." Finally, as Bradford himself points out, "the last four portraits [in the 1926 edition] are elaborate specimens of psychography working consciously, and the last two are as finished psychographs as it is in my power to produce."[2]

The book exists in two different editions. In the 1917 (Dodd, Mead) edition, the contents are as follows (the date of composition is added to each title to enable the reader to check more easily upon changes and developments): "Psychography" (1915), "The Poetry of Donne" (1892), "A Pessimist Poet" (Leopardi) (1893),

"Anthony Trollope" (1901), "An Odd Sort of Popular Book" (Burton's *Anatomy of Melancholy*) (1902), "Alexandre Dumas" (1908), "The Novel a Thousand Years Ago" (1909), "A Great English Portrait Painter" (Clarendon) (1911), "Letters of a Roman Gentleman" (Pliny the Younger) (1912), "Ovid among the Goths" (1913), and "Portrait of a Saint" (Francis of Sales) (1913).

"The Novel a Thousand Years Ago" is the only paper that Bradford chose to omit from the 1926 (Houghton Mifflin) edition, no doubt because it has nothing to do with psychography. As the first sentence, beginning "Not quite two thousand," indicates, the title is more picturesque than accurate, but the essay is a charming, though rather discursive, discussion of the romances of such writers as Heliodorus, Chariton, Longus, and Tatius, with considerable attention to their anticipations of more recent writers. The reader who knows only *Daphnis and Chloe* may well be tempted to read more widely.

But the 1926 edition added three papers: "Walter Pater" (1888), after "Psychography"; "A French Lamb" (Jules Lemaître) (1909), after "Alexandre Dumas"; and "A Gentleman of Athens" (Xenophon) (1911), after "A Great English Portrait Painter."

"Walter Pater," written when the author was twenty-five and his subject still living and producing, discusses the three books then available: *The Renaissance, Marius the Epicurean,* and *Imaginary Portraits.* The study of Donne is chiefly remarkable for having been written before the Donne revival, when his poems were still terra incognita to most readers. Bradford saw Donne's work as "the passionate expression of one of the noblest, tenderest, broadest, and deepest natures that ever received the gift of genius"; his discussion embraces specificity, but he was also capable of impressive, informed generalization.

Psychography first appears at the beginning of the Leopardi, whose Section I might well be the first, orientational, biographical section of a full-fledged psychograph. Section II deals with Leopardi's scholarship, and Section III considers him as a man of letters, but the interest in character delineation persists throughout. The succeeding papers from the Trollope through the Lemaître weave back and forth between description and evaluation of the work and commentary on the personality; in the Burton, the emphasis is on the work, as the title shows. Contrasts and comparisons involving many writers, in many times and countries, abound. Of Trollope Bradford remarks that "he accomplishes with Titanic effort what Shakespeare, Fielding, Miss Austen, Thackeray, and Dickens do with divine ease and unerring instinct," which must be very nearly the only kind thing he ever said about Dickens. If his enthusiasm over Trollope's hunting scenes seems surprising, it is only one more example of his ability to respond to the interests of subjects wholly unlike himself. The study of Dumas is generous toward both man and writer and remarkable for the author's ability to understand the fine qualities which coexisted with both extraordinarily naive egotism and a flagrant disregard of what a New England writer might be expected to regard as imperative moral principles. Because of its preoccupation with an art his commentator shares with the subject, the study of Clarendon is the most professional in the volume; it shows knowledge of Burnet and Lauderdale as well as Clarendon and includes many references to Tacitus and Saint-Simon.

It seems curious that of the four climactic papers in *A Naturalist of Souls*, the first three should, alone among Bradford's portraits, deal with classical subjects. The title "Ovid among the Goths" comes from *As You Like It*, and Bradford himself called attention to its inaccuracy, since it was to "Tomi, a little colony, half Greek, half barbarian, on the Black Sea, near the mouth of the Danube" that Ovid was exiled. To the extent that the study is focused upon this period in the subject's life, it is more specialized than the others, but the concentration is not complete. Xenophon is called "one of the most sweetly, most wholesomely religious natures that ever lived," and the modern reader of "Letters of a Roman Gentleman" is likely to be pulled up sharply and enviously by the opening sentence, which begins, "To us who dwell in settled peace." With all three of the classical subjects, however, the reader must feel strongly the absence of the memorabilia which the writer would have had available in studying more modern figures.

The portrait of Saint Francis of Sales may seem specialized, too, in its concentration upon the subject as a shepherd of souls, but after all this was his life, and certainly Bradford brings in many more general "human" qualities. There is one priceless quotation which has lost nothing since either Francis wrote it or Bradford quoted it. One of the saint's penitents, worried about whether it was right for her to follow the current fashion of powdering her hair, sent him a message imploring his counsel. "Tell her to powder her hair, if she likes," he replied, "so long as her heart is right; for the thing is not worth so much bothering about, Don't get your thoughts entangled among these spider-webs. The hairs of this girl's spirit are more snarled up than those of her head."

The Civil War Trilogy: *Lee the American* (1912); *Confederate Portraits* (1914); *Union Portraits* (1916)

Bradford claimed to have spent fifteen years on his Civil War books, ten of them on Lee,[3] and *Lee the American* was his first published volume of psychography. Its individual chapters attracted considerable attention when published serially in the *Atlantic Monthly*, the *South Atlantic Quarterly*, and the *Sewanee Review* between 1910 and 1912, and the book was one of his most successful, being welcomed with special enthusiasm in the South, where considerable pleasure and surprise was felt that a New Englander could respond with such warmth to the great hero of the Confederacy.

The body of the book comprises eleven chapters: "Lee Before the War," "The Great Decision," "Lee and Davis," "Lee and the Confederate Government," "Lee and His Army," "Lee and Jackson," "Lee in Battle," "Lee as a General," "Lee's Social and Domestic Life," "Lee's Spiritual Life," and "Lee after the War."

It will be clear at once that what we have here is a much less highly integrated psychograph than the author was later to achieve; indeed he himself once spoke of the book as "a series of studies on Lee." Remnants of the chronological method of conventional biography survive at both the beginning and the end, and in the chapters on "Lee and Davis" and "Lee and Jackson" the focus is almost as much on the others as on Lee. Transitions are sometimes awkward, and the introduction of quotations less gracefully managed than in later years; neither is their application always entirely clear and obvious.

The second chapter contains an elaborate discussion of whether Lee was right or wrong when he cast his lot with Virginia rather than the Union, which culminates in the author's astonishing statement that "in the certainly most improbable, but perhaps not wholly impossible, contingency of a future sectional separation in this country, however much I might disapprove of such separation and its causes, I should myself be first, last, and always a son and subject of New England and of Massachusetts."[4] None of this is, strictly speaking, psychography, and there is much more discussion of general ideas for their own sake in the Civil War books than Bradford later permitted himself; there is even, for a layman, considerable attention paid to military strategy.

Bradford is nearly always sympathetic toward his subjects, but his expressions of his admiration for Lee are franker and probably more intrusive than similiar passages elsewhere. The best general summary of Lee's virtues is perhaps that in *Confederate Portraits*:[5]

He had courage without bluster, dignity without arrogance, reserve without haughtiness, tranquility without sloth. A soldier in all his regal bearing, in every fibre of his body, his character was far larger than is essential to the profession of arms. In the great decisions of life he guided his action by what seemed to him the principles of duty, and by these only.

But Bradford is even more personal in Lee's own book:

It is an advantage to have a subject like Lee that one cannot help loving. . . . I have loved him, and I may say that his influence upon my life, though I came to know him late, has been as deep and as inspiring as any I have ever known. If I convey but a little of that influence to others who will feel it as I have, I shall be more than satisfied.

Yet he deplores idolatry as Ben Jonson deplored Shakespeare worship and regrets the growth of a "Lee legend." Late in life he was even to say that much as he admired Lee, he never felt really close to him. He cites testimony against him, even as a general, and grants that some of his nobility was policy. He was fussy and not very approachable. He had no deep interest in either art or science. His letters are colorless and undistinguished, and we have probably lost very little by his failure to write his memoirs. As an educator after the war, he was surprisingly liberal in some aspects and a martinet in others. "About many things we shall never know what he really thought." He asked very little for himself at any time; what then did he mean by saying of his daughter that, like him, she was always wanting something? And what does it show about this uncommonly gentle warrior that at Fredericksburg he should have remarked, "It is well that war is so terrible, or else we might grow too fond of it?"?[6]

There are four generals in *Confederate Portraits*—Joseph E. Johnston, J. E. B. Stuart, James Longstreet, and P. G. T. Beauregard—and one "Rear Admiral" or privateer, Raphael Semmes. Alexander H. Stephens was Vice President of the Confederacy, and Judah P. Benjamin held several Cabinet posts. Robert Toombs served in both military and civil capacities, but his service in the second field was the more important.

In the Preface the author apologizes for what some readers may consider his harshness, and it is true that only the Stuart and Stephens portraits are wholly admiring in tone. The studies of all the generals except Stuart are essentially studies in failure, the whole first part of the Johnston being devoted to a discussion of what was wrong with him and why he did not accomplish more. Aside from his faults as a commander, the answer is sought in his "schoolboy petulance" and "constant attitude of disapproval, of fault-finding, of resentment even approaching sullenness," and the problem becomes that of reconciling these things with his charm and amiability in personal relationships. Though both aspects are adequately described, Bradford does little to reconcile them, and the net result is an impression of incompleteness.

Longstreet and Beauregard are both given credit for honest patriotism, but both were handicapped by vanity, jealousy, and an overdeveloped tendency to criticize. Beauregard had too a weakness for devising elaborate plans to meet contingencies which never developed; Davis called it "driveling on possibilities," and the phrase haunted Bradford. Stuart, on the other hand, was a kind of D'Artagnan. Bradford was always remarkable for his ability to understand and sympathize with persons wholly unlike himself (in this case, exceptional purity in personal conduct would seem to be the only outstanding trait they shared), and the author is quite carried away by his subject's exuberance, his laughter and song, and his genuine joy in life. He cannot deny that Stuart's reports were flowery, yet he declares he loves them. He does not, however, deny the man's limitations, especially on the intellectual side ("Again and again he reminds me of a boy playing soldiers"), and he felt that he was fortunate in being killed at thirty-one.

The portrait of Semmes has the most self-indulgent beginning of any Bradford wrote. He opens with a playful speculation about names, suggested by but not limited to his subject's, and proceeds to develop his own delighted boyhood conception of Semmes as a pirate. Psychography properly speaking does not begin until the ninth page of a twenty-eight-page study, after which we learn that, though capable of coarseness, Semmes had elements of the Christian gentleman about him. The odor of piracy is not wholly blown away, however, and one gets the impression that the author rather relished it.

Stephens was "a figure of commanding purity, sincerity, distinction, and patriotism," but even here contradictions are prominent: physical frailty combined with unimpeachable courage and tremendous spiritual energy, melancholy coupled with genuine humanity and kindness, and much besides. There is an abundance of paradox too about the "unpardoned, unreconstructed, unrepentant rebel" Toombs, whose achievements, like those of the generals, seem out of proportion to his apparent gifts. He was a fighter by temperament whose great defect was that he never learned discipline, yet, in many crises and on many issues, his voice was for peace and conciliation. Benjamin displeased Bradford by destroying all the records he could lay his hands on, and his interpreter admits that he began work with a certain prejudice against him. He sifts the evidence that has survived in an attempt to discover whether the many charges that were made against Benjamin can be justified and emerges with the conclusion that his character was "respectable, if not unexceptionable, but his ability mediocre." Though he was courteous—some said oleaginous—in social relations, his Malvolio-like smile indicated "easy-going egotism," not "heroic fortitude." He worked earnestly, but nothing went very deep with him. and when the war ended, it was over.

At the suggestion of Ellery Sedgwick, and rather against his own preference, Bradford used for the first time in *Union Portraits* the numbered divisions within each paper which appeared in nearly all his subsequent work, and this apparently both accented his structure and made for easier reading. Here are five generals—George B. McClellan, Joseph Hooker, George Gordon Meade, George Henry Thomas, and William T. Sherman;[7] two Cabinet officers—Edwin M. Stanton and William H. Seward; one senator—Charles Sumner; and one journalist—Samuel Bowles.

The first three of the military portraits are again largely studies in failure. All are largely devoted to the subjects in their professional capacity, and there is much examination of testimony for and against them. "He was not much besides a soldier," writes Bradford of Hooker; "and even as a soldier he was not quite as brilliant as he thought he was." McClellan's self-exaltation was nearly maniacal. Hooker could write that "the enemy is in my power, and God Almighty cannot deprive me of them," upon which Bradford comments that "such words as these suggest the Nemesis of great tragedy and give an enthralling interest to the dramatic story of the man who uttered them." Meade's case is different. The victor of Gettysburg was a delicate, modest man, "a quiet scholar who fought as he did problems in arithmetic" and found his job distasteful. But he had no spirit of adventure, became irascible under pressure, and was not popular with his men.

Thomas, on the other hand, did take "a real human joy in fighting and victory," but the great interest of his career inheres in his being the only Southerner among Bradford's generals who fought for the Union. The writer begins with ten pages of speculation as to the reasons for this. Next we explore Thomas's reserve and his freedom from the overconfidence, bluster, and jealousy we have seen in some of the other generals, North and South. The advantages and disadvantages of his reserve, poise, and self-control are set forth, and the view that he was cold and stolid is refuted. The paper ends with the conclusion that Virginia produced the noblest soldier who fought for the North as well as the noblest who fought for the South.

The portrait of Sherman, who marched from Atlanta to the sea, begins by contrasting his freedom in self-revelation with Thomas's reserve, but Section I is devoted to his restless activity, while Section II develops an activity of the mind to match that of the body. Sherman made war like a man of business, doing whatever needed to be done, but taking no special pleasure in fighting for its own sake. Though not personally cruel, "he viewed slaughter with indifference when the necessities of business required it," saying that "in war you can't help yourselves, and the only possible remedy is to stop war." Though not "a mere machine man, without nerves or emotions," he did lack "atmosphere" and "that something of depth and mystery" we find in Lincoln.

Among the civilians', Stanton's is an especially well balanced portrait. The outrageous rudeness and harshness of the Secretary of War must have made him one of the most unpleasant men who ever lived, and Bradford does full justice to this aspect, after which he proceeds to develop the "wonderful depths of emotion and nervous sensibility" that the man possessed, leaving the reader not excusing the rudeness yet forced to admit that Stanton cannot be judged by reference to it alone. In the last section on the secretary's general intellectual qualities, limitations again appear, but the portrait ends on an admiring, conciliatory note. Seward, on the other hand, Bradford sees as an altogether amiable man of no great depth. He was not an idealist even on the slavery issue, and his famous discovery of a "Higher Law" than the Constitution probably surprised him as much as anybody else. More "the clever advocate than the great statesman," he was also "deft, patriotic, and eminently successful." The final section develops, at least suggestively, the thesis that his contradictions and complexities can be explained by the assumption that his temperament was that of an artist.

Charles Sumner, per contra, was the advocate of causes par excellence, and, in the slavery crisis, the voice of the moral law; but Bradford does not credit him with much more depth than Seward. Gideon Welles called his philanthropy "ideal, book philanthropy," and he himself disclaimed religious feeling. Though not selfish nor self-seeking, he was tremendously self-centered and self-satisfied, and despite the devotion of numerous friends, including Longfellow, he was a humorless pedant who posed even when alone. The study of the famous editor of the *Springfield Republican*, Samuel Bowles, has much on journalism and its growing importance in Civil War America, after which we turn to Bowles's social and intellectual qualities, closing with a study of the driving, restless temperament which killed him at fifty-two.

Since Bradford's skill as psychographer never ceased to develop, it should go without saying that many of his later portraits are more consummately done than those in the Civil War trilogy. Moreover, the writers and artists to whom he so often later devoted himself had considerably more substance than the men of action with whom he dealt here. The greatest shortcoming of the Civil War books, however, is that Bradford never faces, or even shows himself aware of, the war problem. Having observed in the Thomas that "a man's conscience is, of course, higher than his military duty," he adds weakly that "the instances where the two should be separated are very rare indeed."[8] Interestingly enough, this matter is most troublesome in connection with Lee himself. Here was one of the most high-minded and winning of human beings, yet he owes his fame to having set thousands of his fellow countrymen to slaughtering each other. Bradford quotes two of Lee's own immensely suggestive utterances on this point but discusses neither of them: "The great mistake of my life was taking a military education" and "For my own part, I much enjoy the charms of civil life, and find too late that I have wasted the best part of my existence."

On the other hand, Bradford was never to achieve a more impressive ending than that of *Lee the American*, where he tells his reader that he wished to do the book partly because, in a country which worships success, Lee was a man who remains great although he failed, who believed that "human virtue should be equal to human calamity" and proved that it could be. The final words are devoted to this incomparable and beautifully told anecdote about Lee's postwar days as president of a small southern college:

A young sophomore was once summoned to the president's office and gently admonished that only patience and industry would prevent the failure that would inevitably come to him through college and through life.

"But, General, you failed," remarked the sophomore, with the inconceivable ineptitude of sophomores.

"I hope that you may be more fortunate than I," was the tranquil answer.

Literature can add nothing to that.

The Distaff Side: *Portraits of Women* (1916); *Portraits of American Women* (1919); *Wives* (1925); *Daughters of Eve* (1930)

Portraits of Women was conceived as "preliminary studies or sketches" for several volumes of psychographs of American women which Bradford planned to have follow his Civil War books. It was a handsome volume, both outside and in; the elegant pale blue cover decorated with a drawing of a lady's fan and graceful lettering, enclosed within an elaborate gold border, was eminently suited to the contents. Bradford himself thought it superior to its immediate successor and was always inclined to resent its modest sale, though he admitted that it was not planned "deliberately as a whole" but had "grown in a rather haphazard way."[9] He wrote it in odds and ends of time while mainly occupied with the Civil War trilogy, "merely gathering what I could from such correspondence and gossip as came in my way. To be sure, they were all subjects that I had long been more or less familiar with."[10] It is the only one of his books which contains nine portraits, and it lacks bibliography, annotations, index, and formal divisions within each paper. Not surprisingly, its organization of materials, while not rambling, is considerably less schematic than in most of the later portraits. An interesting passage in the Preface explains the necessity when portraying women

of dealing with exceptions rather than with average personages. The psychographer must have abundant material, and usually it is women who have lived exceptional lives that leave such material behind them. The psychography of queens and artists and authors and saints is little, if any, more interesting than that of your mother or mine, or of the first shopgirl we meet. I would paint the shopgirl's portrait with the greatest pleasure, but the material is lacking.

The subjects are Lady Mary Wortley Montagu, Lady Holland, Jane Austen, Fanny Burney, Mrs. Samuel Pepys, Madame de Sévigné, Madame du Deffand, Madame de Choiseul, and Eugénie de Guérin. The first four were English, the last four French, with Mrs. Pepys, as the French wife of an Englishman, straddling both groups. The nine lives center on the late eighteenth and early nineteenth centuries. Lady Mary was born in the seventeenth and lived past the middle of the eighteenth. The short life of Elizabeth Pepys was passed wholly during the mid-seventeenth and that of Eugénie de Guérin in the first half of the nineteenth. Jane Austen and Fanny Burney were novelists. We know Mrs. Pepys only through her husband's diary (the writer's problem here anticipated those he faced later, on a larger scale, in *Wives*). Lady Holland and Eugénie de Guérin kept journals, as did the novelist Burney. The others are known mainly as letter writers.

Bradford begins his study of Lady Mary Wortley Montagu with her sharp tongue, then proceeds to modify our initial impression. But even after the other aspects have been duly surveyed, she remains "too calm," "not quite the woman, even in her malice." Altogether, she was "not a winning figure, but a solid one, who, with many oddities, treads earth firmly, and makes life seem respectable, if not bewitching."

The study of Lady Holland is no more sympathetic. It opens with an account of the Holland salon, one of the rare English examples, and this section contains what is probably Bradford's longest quotation, an extract from Macaulay, all the more striking in context because it concerns Lord Holland more than his wife. From here we proceed to the testimony against Lady Holland as a rude, dominating woman whose acts crushed and whose speeches stung. Next, by contrast, we see her as she saw herself, in her journal, "complete, and human, and not unlovely." After a brief summary of her life and general interests, the paper ends with testimonies from others in her favor, to balance the unfavorable views presented at the beginning. "May we not accept Greville's dictum that she was a very strange woman, adding that, after all, she played the role of a great lady in not unseemly fashion?"

Jane Austen is the only one of his subjects in this book that Bradford could have expected his readers to know much about in advance. After having established her provenance, he gives much attention to her mockery, citing his evidence first from her books, then from her letters. Thence he proceeds to his second theme, finding warm humanity under the "demure demeanor" and "an infinite fund of tenderness, a warm, loving, hoping, earnest heart," especially in familial relationships. Yet, in the final analysis, it remains true that though Jane Austen loved mankind in general, or at least took great interest in it, she found "most individual specimens unattractive and even contemptible."

Fanny Burney's life experience is described in greater detail than is usual with Bradford. But he believes the famous diary, which is the principal source for the study of her character, tells more about the observed than the observer, and that even in dealing with others, she is more vivid on external details than essentials of character. Unlike Jane Austen's, her "views of humanity do more credit to her heart than to her head," and the milk of human kindness "oozes from every pore." Her apparently admirable control may well indicate no more than the absence of strong emotion. "She was always flying out of life to preserve it—in syrup."

The portrait of Mrs. Pepys is one of the simplest in the whole Bradford gallery and, within its limitations, admirably organized. It begins with two paragraphs of generalization on the difficulty of portraying ordinary women whose lives have not been chronicled apart from their husbands'. Brief consideration follows of the lady's appearance, interest in fashion, accomplishments or lack of them, domestic management, social life, theater-going, morals, "faults of temper, faults of tongue." The curtain comes down on the difficulty of probing her attitude toward both God and her husband and commentary on their life together, including the problems posed by Pepy's well-known infidelities.

But the four French portraits are the heart of the book. Here are two extraordinarily charming women—Madame de Sévigné and Madame de Choiseul; one near-saint—Eugénie de Guérin; and one fascinating problem—Madame de Deffand. The Sévigné begins with a literary judgment and a comment on the character of the lady's letters and their historical significance; surely they deserve all Bradford's praise, as does their writer—"a sweetly rounded nature, one of the most so, one of the most sane, normal, human women that have left the record of their souls for the careful study of posterity." Abundant testimony establishes the equal worth of Madame de Choiseul, who lived through the French Revolution but might easily have been guillotined; she "knew all the good of life and all the evil. Beauty, rank, wealth, love, honor, exile, ruin, and disaster were all hers. And through them all she remained the same simple, gentle, loyal, heroic figure, admirable if a woman ever was, and memorable if the highest charm backed by the strongest character are indeed worth remembering." Yet neither portrait partakes of hagiography. Madame de Choiseul, sensitive to all else, would seem to have been impervious to religious feeling, and Madame de Sévigné's beautiful normality cracks in her obsessive devotion to her daughter.[11]

Eugénie de Guérin lived almost as "eremetical" a life as Emily Dickinson. God was her all-absorbing passion, for even her adoration of her brother Maurice was, in a measure, subsumed by it, through her agonizing over his salvation. But Bradford always remembers Sainte-Beuve's caution—"Let us not be afraid to surprise the human heart naked—even in the saints." Eugénie was not without literary ambition; neither does she seem to have been completely free from what Anatole France called *"la douceur imperieuse des saintes,"* nor yet, despite her passion for God, from a touch of the ennui which ravaged the life of Madame du Deffand.

The latter, surely the most complicated person in the book, yields a portrait unique in the Bradford gallery. He introduces her to us as "a blind, infirm old woman," with "but one fixed thought, one feeling, one misfortune, one regret, that ever I was born," then flashes back to the irregular youth we need to keep in mind if we would understand her later disillusionment. She had no interest in nature nor learning nor politics nor art nor music and only flirted with religion. "So you set her down as a cold, barren, dead old woman, and think you have heard enough of her. But there is more and of singular interest." She had "indomitable nervous energy" and "French wit." She was "frank, straightforward, and sincere," a dreamer, a disappointed idealist whose natural tendency was to trust. "She was capable of keen and passionate sympathy, and she held kindness to be a great and most estimable virtue." Above all, she was hungry for love. "Everybody loves after his own manner; I have only one way of loving, infinitely, or not at all." And finally she poured out all her passion at the feet of, among all people, that cold, supersophisticated Englishman Horace Walpole, who was sufficiently embarrassed by it to beg her to destroy his letters. It lasted for eleven years, and she died "with this final illusion like the cross in her hands and the sacred wafer at her lips. You think she was pitiably infatuated. Perhaps she was. But it was an infatuation that not only furnished the clue to her whole life, but in a manner sanctified it."

Portraits of American Women might almost, as the author was aware, have been called "Portraits of New England Women," since of its eight subjects only Frances Willard did not hail from that region. There are four writers—Harriet Beecher Stowe, Margaret Fuller, Louisa May Alcott, and Emily Dickinson; one educator—Mary Lyon; one reformer—Frances Willard; and one First Lady—

Abigail Adams. In a class by herself is the author's great-aunt, Sarah Alden Bradford Ripley (1793–1867), one of the learned ladies of her time, who was studied largely from private papers.

The Harriet Beecher Stowe has one of Bradford's characteristic quick beginnings:

> She was a little woman, rather plain than beautiful, but with energy, sparkle and vivacity written all over her. I always think of her curls, but they were not curls of coquetry or curls of sentiment, they were just alive, as she was, and danced and quivered when she nodded and glowed.[12]

We proceed to background and achievement, basic equipment, fundamental interests, and the impulse toward expression and reform, in life and in writing. There is some literary criticism in Section IV, and the discussion of Mrs. Stowe's sunny temperament leads to an amusing excursus in which Bradford, taking his key from the unexpected interest in Rubens which he shared with his subject, indulges himself by wondering whether, had she been "a pagan suckled in a creed outworn," she might have followed it with the same proselytizing ardor that she gave to Christianity," and conjures up an image of her, "thyrsus in her hand, undraped in a dainty, if limited, garment of fawnskin, careering over the pastures by the sea, at the head of a Bacchic squadron of middle-aged New England matrons." But after this "piquant, if indecorous," passage, he pays his closing tribute to *Uncle Tom's Cabin* as "one of the greatest moral agencies the world has seen."

"Sarah Margaret Fuller brought the thrill of life wherever she went, though she was only half alive herself." This time Bradford outlines formally in advance, proposing to treat (1) Margaret's social contacts and relations with others; (2) "the intense activity of her intelligence"; and (3) her emotional life—family, friends (especially Emerson), and her lovers, Nathan and Ossoli (there is no indication of the irregularity of her union with the latter at the outset). The paper ends like a chronological biography with the death by drowning of Margaret, her husband, and child in the wreck off Fire Island, and has a fine closing sentence: "She was a woman of marvelous complexity, like all women, and all men, and her complexity strikes you with tenfold force because she went out like a candle when a window is suddenly opened into great night." Yet, in a late letter, Bradford admits he did not care for her.[13]

The psychograph of Louisa May Alcott is also well, though less formally, organized, covering, in order, background and conditioning factors, artistic capacities and temperament, and motivation for writing. She "coined her soul to pad her purse and, incidentally, to give solace to many," thus standing "in excellent company" with Scott, Dumas, Trollope, and others.

The great thinkers, the great poets, the great statesmen, the great religious teachers sway us upward for our good. But they often lead us astray and they always harass us in the process. I do not know that they deserve more of our gratitude than those who make our souls forget by telling us charming stories. Perhaps "Little Women" does not belong in quite the same order as "Rob Roy," or "Les Trois Mousquetaires," or even "Phineas Finn." But it is not an unenviable fate to have gained an honest independence by giving profit and delight to millions. Miss Alcott did it—and Shakespeare.

Bradford once wrote that he thought his Emily Dickinson the best thing he had done.[14] He begins, as befits his subject, with a kind of vision:

One who, as a child, knew Emily Dickinson well and loved her much recollects her most vividly as a white ethereal vision, stepping from her cloistral solitude onto the veranda, daintily unrolling a great length of carpet before her with her foot, strolling down to where the carpet ended among her flowers, then turning back and shutting herself out of the world.

Then he interprets the vision: "It is just so that we must think of her as coming into the larger world of thought," and, after a brief reference to background, he announces his method of procedure: "We will use the letters to advance with humdrum steps and now

and then get a flash of illumination from the verses." Section II
deals with her human contacts, with a light, glancing reference to
love (Charles Wadsworth's name is not mentioned). There is some
comment on the poetry in Section III, but this is not developed.
An interesting value judgment defends Emily against the charge
that her "dwelling with God and with that which abideth, is
selfish." At the end we return to the vision with which we began
and the loveliest of the songs sung by Emily's "brothers," the clowns
of Shakespeare:

> When that I was and a little, tiny boy,
>   With heigh-ho, the wind and the rain. . . .

Bradford said that he loved Emily and Mrs. Ripley, Mary Lyon
moderately, and Mrs. Stowe, Miss Alcott, and Frances Willard not
at all.[15] The portrait of Mary Lyon is concerned almost wholly with
education—the subject's struggle to secure it for herself, her effort
to bring it to others, and her administration of affairs at Mount
Holyoke—and the author editorializes openly about educational
methods and ideals. Though he was horrified by the hellfire and
damnation sermons Mary Lyon preached to adolescent girls, Bradford sympathized heartily with her desire not merely to feed them
information but to inspire them "to live for God and do something."
Abigail Adams seems to have attracted him less, for he finds it
necessary rather to labor the point that she was "a woman and a
lover," even "a shifting, varying mercurial creature, as perhaps we
all are, but she certainly more than many of us." She is shown not
merely in her personal and domestic aspects but also in relation to
her husband's career as the second President of the United States,
and there is a mini-portrait of him, stressing his egotism, sensitive-
ness, and lack of social charm, which gives occasion for one of
Bradford's priceless comments. When Adams scolds his wife and
announces his intention to scold "again and again" because he considers it his duty, the author slyly remarks, "Perhaps a husband to
whom scolding is a duty is even worse than one to whom it is a
pleasure."

Mrs. Ripley's claim upon our attention is established through testimonies to her learning from Senator Hoar, President Everett, and Professor Child. She was remarkable chiefly for the wide range of her intellectual interests, developed largely without guidance in a day when few women paid much attention to such things. Her greatest interests were philosophy and metaphysics, which led her at last, clergyman's wife though she was, to "a complete, profound, and all-involving intellectual skepticism." Yet her limitations are as remarkable as her achievements. She had no "creative, original intelligence," no literary ambition, no aesthetic passions, no interest in contemporary events. She did not even have any real desire to teach, though she did teach when it became necessary and did it well. But what might otherwise have been a mere gluttonous hunger for acquisition was saved by her sweet human warmth and friendliness. "I may be childish," she said in her old age, "but there are no limits to love." Structurally, her grandnephew's study of her is, for him, oddly chronological: he gives her to us first in youth, then in old age, "because in fairness I should end with the ripe perfection of her middle years."

This leaves Frances Willard, the founder of the Woman's Christian Temperance Union. Bradford's first impression of her was favorable, but he soon found that she repelled him and even worried about whether he might bring the wrath of the WCTU down upon both the *Atlantic Monthly* and himself, and in the introductory essay to *Wives*, he would write, "She was a splendid woman, only I could not bear her, would have walked miles to avoid meeting her, and that got into my portrait too."

Yet the study is eminently fair and dispassionate and structurally perhaps the most interesting in the book. It has a good opening sentence: "She had the great West behind her; its sky and its distances, its fresh vigor and unexampled joy," and this is followed by an effective summary of Miss Willard's life experience and personality traits, which leads in turn to the quotation which strikes Bradford's keynote: "The chief wonder of my life is that I dare to have so good a time, both physically, mentally, and religiously." Next he describes her work, first in its effect upon others and then upon herself. What a wonderful story is that of the hostess who thoughtlessly offered her a glass of wine. "The blood flashed in cheek and brow as I said to her, 'Madam, two hundred thousand women would lose something of their faith in humanity if I should drink a drop of wine.'" And Bradford comments: "Think what it must be to feel the eyes of two hundred thousand women fixed upon you from the time you wake till the time you sleep again. That is the way Miss Willard lived."[16]

Bradford's third book about women, *Wives* (1925), differed from its predecessors in being devoted to women who would never have been heard of save that they happened to marry famous or infamous men. In *Damaged Souls* (1923) he had already expressed his admiration for Mrs. Benjamin F. Butler and his wish that he were studying her rather than him. He now did just this, adding studies of Mrs. Benedict Arnold and Theodosia Burr, whose husband and father respectively were both damaged, and of Mrs. James G. Blaine, whose husband had appeared in *American Portraits, 1875– 1900* (1922). The other three ladies—Dolly Madison, Mrs. Jefferson Davis, and Mrs. Lincoln—had husbands who had not "sat" to Bradford, but the last two stood against the Civil War background he knew so well.[17]

The publication of *Wives* followed hard upon that of *Bare Souls* (1924), and there could not be a sharper contrast than that between the two. *Bare Souls* presented the writer the challenge of superb material, the matchless self-revelation of a group of writers, several of whom touched genius. Except for Mrs. Butler, the material for *Wives* was scattered and scanty and the problem often that of determining the woman's traits from what had been written about her husband. The character of Mrs. Davis, however, was largely inferred from the book she herself wrote about Davis, while with Mrs. Lincoln "there was the necessity of deducing her almost entirely from the report of others, report so slippery and uncertain that you never felt any real confidence that you were getting near the facts."[18] "In short," wrote Bradford slyly, "I cannot ask my readers to give implicit belief to anything I may say about Mrs. Lincoln, for I believe very little of it myself."[19]

These last two are the least attractive women in the book. Mrs. Davis was indeed intelligent, solid, substantial, efficient, and respectworthy, but she had "a quick, ill-regulated, imperious nature." The last two sections of her portrait deal with her as a wife and as the wife of a president, and there is some consideration of Davis himself. Mrs. Lincoln Bradford regarded as "a very disagreeable person, and the only interest of her is to show how she worked on Lincoln."[20] Yet the portrait, despite lacunae, achieves an admirably comprehensive coverage of what is known or can reasonably be conjectured. What we know about her own interests (Section I), her "external life" (II), and her relations with her husband (III), though not all embracing, is certainly not negligible. The last two sections are more tentative but no less interesting. "Having thus analyzed, with delightful inconclusiveness, the conjugal affection of the Lincolns, we may consider with equal inconclusiveness, the important question of Mrs. Lincoln's influence over her husband." And, again, "As this portrait is mainly made up of questions that cannot be answered, we might as well conclude with the most unanswerable of all, would Lincoln's career have been different, for better or worse, if he had married a different wife?" Bradford did not think so; Lincoln was in no sense a woman's man. As for her influence, she cannot have had much, nor is it likely that there was "much spiritual sympathy between her and her husband." Yet, except for its ending, the marriage was hardly a tragedy. "It was probably an every-day marriage, with some rather dark spots in it, but hardly so bad as has been represented."

The study of Peggy Shippen Arnold is concerned largely with whether she was, as Aaron Burr claimed, involved in her husband's treason; Bradford rejected this view. The opening paragraphs present her as a Greek tragic heroine, indicate her background and personality briefly, and proceed to the circumstances of her marriage. Up to the end of Section II we have not had a single quotation from her. Part III draws upon the letters she wrote her father and others during her years in England to establish the kind of woman she was. That she loved Arnold there is no doubt, but we have no word from her concerning his treason.

Dolly Madison was a happy, "centrifugal" spirit, and her letters do not suggest that she had much of an inner life. Her social proclivities are heavily stressed, but both her famous attractiveness and her gaucherie (as in her snuff-taking) are passed over lightly. The paper ends on a positive and admiring note. "I always thought better of *myself*," said one of her nieces, "when I had been with Aunt Dolly."

The opening section of the Theodosia Burr is somewhat discursive. Sections II and III deal with her mainly as wife and mother, while Section IV moves up to the all-important matter of her relations with her father Aaron Burr, with equal attention to their devotion to each other and his amazing shamelessness in keeping nothing from her, not even his disreputable erotic adventures. Theodosia, who apparently sympathized with him even in his wild Mexican scheme, loved her father "for his gentleness, for his thoughtfulness, for what seemed to her his unselfishness and consideration, and because he liked to see people happy." In other words, a "superb woman, with an intellect as keen as her character was lofty, made an idol" of a bad man who was also a small man, "an abominable reprobate" who stands "branded with eternal ignominy and with the mark of Cain upon his forehead." This puzzled Bradford as it puzzles us, and he got no further toward explaining it than to find "a certain similarity" between father and daughter "in their eternal childlikeness. . . . The world, to both of them, was instinctively a matter of pretty things."

But the two most remarkable portraits in *Wives* are those of Sarah Butler and Harriet Blaine. The latter is very interesting structurally, for the author surrounds Mrs. Blaine with concentric circles, seeing her in the world, in her home, in her relations with her husband and, finally, with her own soul.[21] The peculiarity of Sarah Butler's portrait is that virtually all the material is derived from the letters she wrote between 1860 and 1865, which have been printed only in connection with Butler's own much more extensive correspondence. These letters are superb in quality, though limited in extent; if she had less "ease and natural expression" than Harriet Blaine, Mrs. Butler had more "imaginative depth and power" and was a much more charming person. Naturally we see her mainly, though not exclusively, in her relations with her husband, and Bradford passes over the question of how such a woman could have loved such a man on the ground that "we see the love of higher, finer natures just so erring every day," yet, for all his admiration for Sarah Butler, he does not hesitate to point out her shortcomings— "a touch of . . . acerbity" and "just the slightest trace . . . of that lack of higher, finer delicacy" which is so much more prominent in her husband.

Daughters of Eve was the first book in which Bradford used titles, not merely the names of his subjects, for his chapter headings: "Eve in the Apple-Orchard: Ninon de Lenclos," "Eve as Dove and Serpent: Madame de Maintenon," "Eve and Almighty God: Madame Guyon," "Eve and Adam: Mademoiselle de Lespinasse," "Eve Enthroned: Catherine the Great," "Eve and the Pen: George Sand," and "Eve in the Spotlight: Sarah Bernhardt."

All the subjects were French except Catherine the Great, who was a German, though she ruled Russia. Ninon, de Maintenon, and Guyon were seventeenth-century figures who lived over into the eighteenth. Julie de Lespinasse and Catherine the Great belonged to the eighteenth century altogether. George Sand was of the nineteenth century, as was Sarah Bernhardt mainly, though she did not die until 1923.

Bradford conceived of *Daughters of Eve* late in 1927. Excited by the success of *Damaged Souls*, he thought of doing "women of conspicuous and sensational quality, who if not exactly damaged souls themselves, should at least match the men who were." A correspondent had already suggested Ninon, and he thought also of Maintenon and Catherine, "mixed, say, with Catherine of Siena and Saint Teresa,"[22] this last an idea for character contrast which he would carry out not in the *Daughters* but in the last book published during his lifetime, *Saints and Sinners*. Harpers was still trying to get him away from Houghton Mifflin, but Ferris Greenslet saw the *Daughters* as his most salable item since *Damaged Souls* and even succeeded in arranging for a book club edition with the Book League. Bradford was writing at slightly greater length now

and economically stopping with seven subjects to a volume instead
of the usual eight.

Ninon de Lenclos was of course one of the most famous of
courtesans, and Catherine, George Sand, and Sarah Bernhardt were
all *grandes amoureuses*. Bradford does not exactly justify any of
them, but his attitude is not priggish. He did hesitate rather charmingly over his study of Ninon; neither he nor his wife could feel
"that it is particularly moral in its drift, since it portrays Ninon in
an eminently favorable, not to say charming light." He was sure
the *Atlantic* would not have printed it in Bliss Perry's time, but
Harper's delightedly featured it now. Still, he was not sure that because times had changed, he wanted to change with them. "Scrupu-
lousness is born in my blood . . . and I shall never altogether get
rid of it. But I will portray human subjects as I find them, no matter
where they lead me."[23] By the time he came to George Sand, he
had capitulated completely. "I find George so delightfully sympathetic, that I admire her personality and enter so fully into her
views in every possible way." And he even adds, "I have known no
woman but my own H[elen] that could equal her"![24]

The paper on Ninon opens very journalistically for Bradford:

> Three hundred years ago Ninon de Lenclos was just such a girl as
> New York breeds to-day by dozens, fearing neither God nor man, dar-
> ing everything, challenging everything, perfectly reckless of the tattered
> conventions of a worn-out morality, mocking the tame taboos of a more
> timid generation, determined to give full development and outlet to
> every power and vigor of the spirit, to suck from life every drop of rich
> and varied sweetness that it can possibly be made to yield.

Her admirable qualities were her excellent manners, her sensibility,
her temperance in eating and drinking, her avoidance of all coarse
dissipation, her scrupulous financial honesty and generosity, and
her fidelity in friendship; what was most remarkable about her was
that she should have been able to crown her abandoned youth with
"an old age of dignity, tranquility, and peace," and if we are inclined to attribute Bradford's wonder over this to New England

Puritanism, we might do well to remember that it had equally impressed the quite unpuritan Sainte-Beuve before him.

The portrait of George Sand is even more frank about sex than the Ninon; what disarmed Bradford here was obviously the maternal element in the lady's amours and the "essential idealism" which ran through all her relationships. This psychograph is unified around a central idea to a larger extent than is usual with Bradford, but it also admits more biography and literary criticism than he generally allows himself; indeed, virtually the whole first section is biography. Catherine the Great, whose amorous exploits are disposed of first, did not, like George Sand, pursue a romantic ideal; hers was a bourgeois, down-to-earth attitude, and her various entanglements were like a series of companionate marriages, displaying no evidence of any consciousness of wrongdoing on her part. Due and discriminating regard is paid also to her political aspects, yet the last paragraph manages to be both condescending and sentimental:

So of the great Empress we may fairly say that, take her for all in all, she was not only great, one of the most energetic, creative, dynamic, feminine personalities that ever existed, she was also in many respects thoroughly lovable, and one may even venture to say that she was good, though she was an Empress and she had her little eccentricities.

Sarah Bernhardt evidently attracted him less, for though he does full justice to her creative spirit, he finds "just the suggestion of something hard and cynical about her, even of something common," at the same time granting that "many of her admirers do not seem to have felt this," and he does not believe "that she really lived very much for any one but herself, or ever much lost her identity in that of anyone else." He gives less attention to her amours than to those of the other women, but he admits that "she loved for love or for character or for position, but not for money" and that her love seems to have "inspired, ennobled, and enriched" those upon whom it was bestowed rather than degrading them.

Julie de Lespinasse ("she was one of the great lovers of the world") is the only other daughter in whom this element seems very important, and Julie knew the agonies of love—"a hideous, magnificent, tragic tumult of volcanic amorous passion"—better than either its ecstasies or indulgences. The latter are indeed disposed of in a single sentence, in which we are told that "in a moment of complete abandonment, she made [to the Comte de Guibert] the last great sacrifice, which she had never made to her former, nobler lover [the Marquis de Mora], and from that hour on her life was a torture of tragedy and nothing else." (Than that "last great sacrifice" surely no greater tribute was ever paid to Puritan morality.) This psychograph is a companion piece to the Madame du Deffand in *Portraits of Women*, for Julie began as the latter's protégée, quarreled with her, and set up a successful rival salon, thus incurring her patroness's lasting enmity. Bradford admitted a certain monotony, a certain wilfulness or subjectivity in the "record of love and wretchedness" which Julie left us, but if human experience is worth knowing and understanding, it has its value. "Let those who have known nothing whatever of the wretchedness or the love throw stones, if they choose."

It is interesting that the two women in whose lives sex would seem to have been least important should also be the least attractive in the book. To be sure, scandal has been whispered about both Madame de Maintenon and Madame Guyon, but Bradford dismisses it in both cases, and it seems odd that the final section of the latter's portrait should be devoted to an analysis of "the mystical longing" and even of "the sex instinct itself" and the connection between the two, for though none of this is really irrelevant, it does take the spotlight off the subject. Madame Guyon sought to subsume all life experience in devotion to God, and Madame de Maintenon, "a poor girl who had kept geese in the fields," married Louis XIV, "the greatest king in the world," thus making one of the most practical and reasonable women that ever lived the heroine of a fairy tale. Was she as free of ambition, as exclusively devoted to her duty, as she claimed? Who can say? In her abundant self-analysis, she generally manages to turn her faults into virtues. Though a king fell in love with her and put the world at her feet, she "attracts us . . . little" and wins "our respect and not our love." And Madame Guyon` is even more of a problem because she aimed higher. In her psychograph, as in her life, everything else is subordinated to her religious experience. But in religionists of her executive type, "the denial of self" means "influencing, controlling, dominating others." What dictator, what tyrant, ever displayed a more monstrous egotism than she when she wrote:

Yet Our Lord, together with all the weakness of childhood, gives me the power of a god over souls; so that with one word I can put them in torment or in peace, according as it may be best for their eternal welfare.

And what blasphemer can have surpassed

The Lord will one day pour forth his pity; he will establish the lines of his empire through me, and the nations will recognize his sovereign power. . . . Yes, I shall be through him the mistress over those who rule, and those who are subject unto none shall be subject unto me by the force of his divine authority, from which they can never escape without escaping from God himself.[25]

An Aborted Series:
American Portraits, 1875–1900 (1922);
As God Made Them (1929); *Biography
and the Human Heart* (1932)

American Portraits, 1875–1900 was designed as the first of a series of volumes covering representative Americans, with four volumes on the nineteenth century, three on the eighteenth, and two on the seventeenth, which Bradford expected to occupy him for the remainder of his days. In the 1875–1900 volume he originally planned to have Mark Twain, Henry Adams, Sidney Lanier, James G. Blaine, Grover Cleveland, Phillips Brooks, James McNeill Whistler, Joseph Jefferson, and Nathaniel Shaler. Brooks and Shaler were dropped, the scientist because Bradford's advisers did not think him sufficiently representative and Brooks because Bradford himself did not find him interesting, and Henry James was added. Ellery Sedgwick wanted William James, too, but Bradford

finally decided against him, being afraid of the metaphysics involved. As the volume finally appeared, then, it included four
writers, two politicians, a painter, and an actor.

The design of the Cleveland reflects the solidity of its subject.
The approach seems a bit negative—"What a comfort it is to find
a statesman who did not succeed by his tongue!"—and the close
is in harmony with this: "A four-square, firm, solid, magnificent
Titan, who could speak the everlasting no, so rare and so essential
to democracy. We still await the genius, even greater than he, who
can speak the everlasting yes." Bradford asks how Cleveland accomplished what he did and answers that he did it by sticking to
his job. His characteristics and interests are analyzed systematically—
qualities of mind, friendships, dealings with money and religion.
The third section sums up both his assets and his disabilities as a
politician, and the fourth tells what he stands for in the record of
American politics.

The organization of the Blaine is somewhat less "regular." It
begins with a discussion of the source value of his wife's letters.
Section I covers his intellectual and aesthetic limitations and his
amusing hypochondria, but Section II does full justice to him as
husband and father and to the charm and magnetism which he
must have possessed, though Bradford admits that his photographs
do not show it: "Indeed, in some of them there is a look about the
eyes that repels." But the last two sections are taken up entirely
with a factual account of the financial operations which, though
nothing was ever proved, raised suspicions which wrecked Blaine's
supreme ambition, to be elected President, and the highly rhetorical
ending is surely Bradford's saddest and most merciless final paragraph:

Such was the great moral tragedy of James Gillespie Blaine. With
pretty much all the virtues, all the graces, all the gifts of genius, he will
be remembered in his country's annals as the man who lost the presidency because he was suspected of financial dishonor.

No wonder the Blaines were angered and grieved. Bradford himself had worried about this paragraph and consulted the historian F. L. Paxson about deleting it, but Paxson had advised that it be retained.

With so admirable and delightful a man as Joseph Jefferson, the psychographer does not have much to do but expound his excellence, and this is exactly what Bradford does—first in connection with his theatrical career, then in his private life. The dream quality which he notes in Mark Twain impresses him here also, and the only oddity of the study is the closing quotation from Calderón which rather distracts the reader's attention from the subject. The much more fantastic Whistler also lends himself to fairly straightforward treatment. The very beginning strikes the keynote:

> The problem with Whistler is to reconcile a great artist with a little man; or, if not a little man, an odd man, an eccentric man, a curious, furious creature, who flitted through the world, making epigrams and enemies, beloved and hated, laughing and laughable, and painting great pictures. He was glorified by his hand and damned by his tongue.

Section I establishes Whistler's fundamental interests and closes on his childlike posing. The very vivid Section II concerns his notorious feuds and quarrels, from which we pass abruptly, in Section III, to "the thoughtful, earnest, even lofty-souled artist" who lived side by side with the petulant, egotistical, self-indulgent child who could never be counted upon for mature, responsible, human behavior except in relation to his work. In the last section, Bradford considers Whistler's personality as revealed in his paintings. While this is certainly legitimate psychographic material, there is as much Bradford in it as Whistler; indeed he admits that he had gone into the matter "perhaps too subtly." Nevertheless, he thought the last pages of the Whistler one of the best things he had done.

The opening of the wholly sympathetic portrait of Sidney Lanier strikes the keynote: "Lanier lived in a spiritual whirlwind until it snuffed him out." He fought in the Civil War, and he fought poverty, disease, and his own temperament. He made thinking as terrible a job as did Lucretius; he himself says, "Thought is carnivorous. It lives on meat. We never have an idea whose existence has not been purchased by the death of some atom of our fleshly tissue." But Bradford is careful to make it clear that Lanier was not a bristly person and that he was capable of being genial and companionable. The last two sections deal with his aims and motives as an artist and with the results of his striving, and the piece ends with a rather disparaging estimate of his poetry. Strictly speaking, there was no need for this in a psychograph, and if it was to be included, one cannot but wonder why it should have been given such a climactic position.

The most serious questions arise in connection with the other three literary portraits. It must be remembered that much scholarly work has been done on Mark Twain, Henry James, and Henry Adams since Bradford wrote and that it is not fair to judge these studies in the full light of what we know now. He begins with a statement of his personal experience with Mark Twain, going back to his boyhood days, and emphasizes the bardic element in Mark's work, that of "the old, epic, popular singer, who gathered up in himself, almost unconsciously, the life and spirit of a whole nation and poured it forth, more as a voice, an instrument, than as a deliberate artist." But much of his emphasis is strongly negative. He gives Mark Twain full credit for personal goodness ("what failures there were in his moral character were those incident to humanity"), but he is keen on his limitations as a thinker ("he seems always like a man discovering things which are perfectly well known to trained thinkers"), he denies him profundity ("even Nature did not touch great depths in him, because they were not there"), he refuses to rank him with the great humorists ("his writing alternates from the violence of unmeaning laughter to the harshness of satire that has no laughter in it"), and he finds the effect of his pessimism and nihilism utterly devastating ("with the wholesale destruction of shams, went, as so often, the destruction of reverence, 'that angel of the world,' as Shakespeare calls it"). Yet, however all this may need to be qualified now, as a work of art Bradford's portrait of Mark Twain ranks with his best. Its organization is less formal, less schematic than much of his work; it is more like a tone poem than a symphony, and it is rich in color, with much of Mark's own great spirit in it. For "whatever view you take of him, if you live with him long, he possesses and obsesses you; for he was a big man and he had a big heart."

Bradford thought his study of Henry James a failure because his subject was "too essentially dead. That is, the essence of my treatment is that his art was the whole of him to such an extent that it not only killed him personally, but killed his interest in life in itself, and so in a sense by killing the matter of his art finally killed even his art."[26] But this was much too severe a judgment not only upon James but also upon Bradford's own work. He begins unerringly: "He was a man whose whole life was in art, and to whom life and art were inextricably one. . . . He lived and thought and felt to write great novels, and he wrote them, novels of an impossible subtlety and complexity, yet too beautiful and too original for men to let them die." Most of the portrait is devoted to James's attitude toward his art and his practice of it, and it is clear that Bradford was overwhelmed by the famous "later manner," though he never falls into the vulgarity and insensitivity concerning it in which many James haters have indulged. He called James "the greatest of American novelists," and he does full justice to his warmth as a man. But he quite fails to discern the depth of commitment to ethical and human values, which were as far from being "only the material, interesting and valuable as furnishing stuff for the absorbing artistic passion to develop all its resources of cunning and cleverness" in his work as in that of any novelist who ever lived.

The Henry Adams is a more complicated matter. It was based almost wholly on *The Education of Henry Adams*, and it is keyed almost entirely to Adams's determination not to permit the universe to educate him. Bradford sees him as essentially a dilettante, incapable of passion or enthusiasm; he does not make an exception even of Adams's delight in Gothic architecture, and he says nothing about his devotion to the Blessed Virgin. Bradford also comes as close to preaching as he ever does when, in his conclusion, he tells us that what Adams needed was to be de-educated, and that if Mary Lyon could have got hold of him and taught him, as she taught her pupils, to "live for God and do something," she "might have solved his problem, though she would have robbed the world of many incomparable phrases."

The truth is that in castigating Adams, Bradford was castigating himself. John Randolph (*Damaged Souls*) is the only other subject in whom he saw himself to the same extent, and he treats Randolph far more sympathetically. This emerges clearly from what Bradford wrote Ellery Sedgwick. Dissatisfied with his paper, he had recalled it from the *Atlantic* for revision, then decided that his revision had accomplished nothing.

The difficulty was much increased for me precisely because I find in myself just the same tendencies that Adams had, the vague, uncertain, half-trifling, half-despairing struggles to fix and precipitate the furious flux of life, in some definite, tangible spiritual formula, instead of adjusting one's self to it by abandoning one's self with subtle receptivity to the perpetual movement about one. I have never succeeded and never shall, any more than he did.[27]

Though Bradford often said that he expected the projected volumes of the American portraits series to be his most enduring monument, he showed considerable reluctance to get back to them after having finished the religious trilogy devoted to Moody, Darwin, and *Life and I*. This was partly because the success of *Damaged Souls* had given him new ideas and a hunger for more exciting subjects, as well as an enlarged public, and partly because his health made it difficult or impossible for him to do the kind of digging in libraries that the American series demanded; neither was his enthusiasm for it increased by the rejection of Henry Clay by the *Atlantic* and of Calhoun by the *Harper's* editors, who also insisted upon making cuts in the Daniel Webster, which they did accept. In 1929 Bradford wrote a correspondent that he only began to write on American subjects in self-defense because people did not care for the French and classical themes which really interested him. "And after sticking to the American topics for fifteen years I am giving them up and going back to Europe again with a real feeling of relief."[28]

In 1925 Bradford expected the 1850-1875 volume of the American series to embrace Longfellow, Whitman, Edwin Booth, Horace Greeley, William Morris Hunt, Francis James Child, Asa Gray, and the "Confederate Pepys," John Beauchamp Jones, and the 1825–1850 volume Webster, Clay, Calhoun, Thoreau, Hawthorne, Poe, and Theodore Parker, possibly also Edwin Forrest. Five years earlier, however, he had intended this volume to comprise Booth, Child, Gray, and Greeley, along with Ben Butler, John Brown, and P. T. Barnum, who ended up in *Damaged Souls*, plus General Grant and Robert G. Ingersoll, whom, like Hawthorne, Thoreau, Poe, Parker, and Forrest, he never did anywhere. Elsewhere he also mentions Jones Very and Henry Ward Beecher. Once he even considered grouping the American portraits topically rather than chronologically.

As the book which became *As God Made Them: Portraits of Some Nineteenth Century Americans* (1929) was finally sent to the publishers, however, it covered Webster, Clay, Calhoun, Greeley, Booth, "Portrait of a Scientist: Asa Gray," and "Portrait of a Scholar: Francis James Child." Because Greenslet did not like the title "American Victorians," Bradford suggested nine other possibilities, of which Greenslet chose the first, *As God Made Them. Biography and the Human Heart*, which appeared posthumously in 1932, took up the five American portraits still uncollected—Longfellow, Whitman, Hunt, Charlotte Cushman, and Jones (now called an American, rather than a Confederate, Pepys)—plus four nonpsychographic items: two articles on biography—"Biography and the Human Heart" and "Biography by Mirror"—from a projected book on biography which had been abandoned when Greenslet lost interest in it; the appreciation of the Salem poet Jones Very which had been Bradford's very first published article, in the *Unitarian Review*, February 1887, and for which he had been paid $7.50; and "The Letters of Horace Walpole," a review of the Toynbee edition, in the *Atlantic*, March 1906, which may best be read as a supplement to the psychograph of Walpole in *Bare Souls*.

As God Made Them is the book in which Bradford established the practice of devoting his second paragraph to a succinct biographical summary; hitherto he had relied for orientation on the chro-

nology prefixed to each portrait. He found Calhoun repellent, liked
Webster moderately, and was charmed by Clay. Yet he found his
job in general tough going. The Webster repays careful study for
its skillful citation of testimony from outside sources and the abundance of the rhetorical devices employed. It is interesting too to see
how all the more serious charges that have been made against Webster are discounted or played down. He had "one of those large,
rich, self-indulgent natures, which work only when there is an in-
centive, not for the pure pleasure of it," and his "love of the sunrise
and habit of five o'clock in the morning work are quite inconsistent
with serious dissipation." For all that, the charges made have been
registered in the reader's mind. There is considerable straight history in connection with Webster's stand on controversial issues involving slavery: Bradford agrees with him and gives him and Clay
credit for postponing the Civil War for ten years, with the result
that we have one nation in America today "instead of two, or half a
dozen, all tearing at each other with mutual jealousies, and the
constant conflicts, and the ruinous standing armies that have af-
flicted Europe."[29]

The portrait of Webster is notable too for one of the most wonderful anecdotes in any of Bradford's psychographs. When the great
man was dying, he gathered his household about him, in the most
approved macabre, nineteenth-century fashion, and, having dictated
a long rhetorical statement, lost consciousness.

When he came to himself again, he looked about eagerly, and ex-
claimed: "Have I—wife, son, doctor, friends, are you all here?—have
I, on this occasion, said anything unworthy of Daniel Webster?" I do
not know many things in history that will beat that for concentrated
human truth. Try to apply that speech to other notable men. Chatham
might have been capable of it. Napoleon, just possibly, though with
his tongue in his cheek. But who can imagine Lincoln staging such a
performance, who can imagine Shakespeare? Shakespeare would have
smiled and said, "nothing human can be unworthy of Shakespeare." In
all the crepuscular utterances of mortality I know of none more magnificent: "Have I—wife, son, doctor, friends, are you all here?—have I,
on this occasion, said anything unworthy of Daniel Webster?" And then

there comes the due wail of Greek choral response: "No, no, dear sir." "No, no, dear sir." And the drama is complete.

Webster furnished the material here. But it was Bradford who had the wit to make superb use of it.

There is a comparable briefer passage in the psychograph of Clay, who became an Episcopalian at the age of seventy:

It appeared that he had never been baptized, and this point was, of course, attended to before confirmation. The ceremony was performed in the family parlor with the aid of a huge cut-glass vessel, which had been presented to the statesman some years before. No biographer hints at such a thing, but it seems to me highly probable that the vessel was a punch-bowl. It could hardly have been meant to hold flowers, and it certainly was not intended for a baptismal font. Baptized at seventy in a punch-bowl! Could there be a more delightful epitome of Kentucky life a century ago?

If this seems too Lytton Strachey–ish for Bradford, we may remind ourselves that he tells us in his very first sentence that Clay was "the most distinctly and warmly human" of his three statesmen. He keeps this note reverberating throughout the rather loosely organized psychograph, which closes on a comparison between the subject and "Clay's inheritor in many respects, the child of his own Kentucky, the supreme embodiment of the Western spirit, the savior of the Union, Abraham Lincoln," thus putting the closing emphasis upon Lincoln rather than Clay, yet glorifying Clay by association. For all that, Bradford was no more impressed by Clay's inner emotional depth than by Webster's. "Goethe said that whenever he had a sorrow he made a poem. When Clay had a sorrow he made a speech." His relations with God were "cordial but not intimate," and when his wife was asked whether it was not a pity that he gambled so much, she replied, "Oh, I don't know. He usually wins."

As for Calhoun, he "expressed great reverence for the Bible, especially when it could be used as an argument for slavery." But since he "seems to have impressed his contemporaries mainly as a thinking machine," Bradford approaches him from this angle, and much of Section I is devoted to his ideas rather than his personality. A later section probes for "breaks and flaws in the systematic, steely completeness" of his "intellectual armor," but none is really shown save the frustrated ambition to be president which he shared with Webster and Clay. The psychograph ends with a long excursus on the Federal Constitution and states rights, including a topical reference to the Sacco-Vanzetti case.

Bradford's portrait of Horace Greeley ends rather disparagingly with the familiar quotation from *Julius Caesar* about the evil that men do living after them and the comment: "Greeley had done no evil or none to speak of, and the good he did, extensive and indisputable as it was, was not of a character to make the world revere his memory." The paper as a whole is considerably more favorable than that, however; if Bradford fully relishes and exploits the editor's many idiosyncrasies, he is deeply interested in him as one of the leading exponents of the typically nineteenth-century force of journalism; nor are either his personal oddities nor his ill-advised and tragic bid for the presidency permitted to reduce him to a figure of fun.

Booth, Child, and Asa Gray all had charm to burn, and Bradford makes no effort to resist it. The beginning of the Booth is one of the most brilliant he ever achieved:

The most real of all human figures are the creations of the imagination. The nearest approach to earthly immortality, to an existence that is not shattered or imperiled by failure or decay, belongs to spirits that have never lived in the flesh, but have been embodied by great artists in dream shapes that have taken enduring hold upon the fancy and the memory of humanity. Helen, Hector, and Achilles, Dido and Aeneas, Hamlet, Lear, Rosalind and Portia live and will live when millions who have known and loved them have been buried and forgotten. To have attached your name to such a figure, as creator, or even as impersonator, is to attach something of its permanence to the fragile nonentity of a trivial creature of clay.

Booth's humanity is explored in connection with both his personal and professional life, but the alcoholism which he completely conquered after the death of his first wife and the dismal tragedy of his second marriage are passed over lightly, and there is no mention anywhere of the excessive smoking which he never conquered nor tried to and which certainly contributed to his death.

The two scholars are much less well known to the general reader than Booth, and the last section of the Gray is a kind of epilogue on the delights of learning. "Music, love, ballads, roses!" were the constituents of the life of Child, the great editor of the English and Scottish popular ballads, though they never crowded out his concern for the public welfare nor a serene, comforting religious faith. Bradford presents him fairly and attractively, with just the right spice of humor and temper: "Ah, what a world—with roses, sunrise and sunset, Shakespeare, Beethoven, brooks, mountains, birds, maids, ballads—why can't it last, why can't everybody have a good share?" The botanist Gray was not wholly unlike him temperamentally, different as their interests were. Except for Darwin, he is the only scientist Bradford ever limned, and he was one of Darwin's great champions in America, himself quite unconvinced of what seemed to Bradford the devastating effects of Darwinism upon religious faith. The psychographer sees Gray, like Darwin, as a noble exemplification of the scientific spirit at its best, and it may well be that he skims over the controversy with Agassiz, who was anti-Darwinian, a bit lightly.

In *Biography and the Human Heart* the portraits of both the poets are excellent. Bradford begins the Longfellow with the famous remark of the senile Emerson at Longfellow's funeral that the man being buried had a beautiful soul, though Emerson had forgotten his name, and the body of the paper is made up of an accumulation of testimony and evidence to support this evaluation. The odd thing about the study is the sharp contrast between the writer's affection and admiration for Longfellow as a man ("one of the most exquisite souls, perhaps the most exquisite I have ever studied")[30] and his low estimate of the poetry. Yet though he quotes the judgment that "anybody could have written it," he quickly rejects it, "because if anybody could have written it, anybody would," and the last paragraph goes far to remove the sting:

It is a great thing to have a beautiful soul. It is a far, far greater thing to leave that soul as an eternal possession and example and inspiration to millions of one's fellow-men.

The problem of interpreting Whitman is crowded with pitfalls which do not arise in connection with Longfellow, but Bradford does not fall into any of them. Though he never uses the word homosexuality, he shows that he is aware of the controversy concerning it in its possible relation to Whitman; he does full justice to both Whitman's egotism and his unselfish service of others, especially in Civil War hospitals; and he is excellent on the paradox involved in his subject's attempting to speak for a people who greatly preferred Longfellow's poetry to his. There is much too which shows that Bradford realized that though in some aspects Whitman does represent a revolt against the genteel tradition, his values differed much less from those of his contemporaries of New England's "flowering" than many persons suppose.

Homosexuality arises again in connection with Charlotte Cushman, where Bradford gives less indication than in the Whitman that he is aware of its presence. He did not find Charlotte "particularly sympathetic or particularly interesting to me, too mannish, and I do not like mannish women, what man does?"[31] He had to take her out of the book he had first thought of as "Souls of American Women" when it became *Wives*, for "she was oppressively a virgin, not to say a virago."[32] But he thought Sedgwick would like his portrait of her and was surprised he did not, and even more so when Mencken rejected it also. He had told Mencken that she was "a rather awful personage, a sort of mixture of Calvin, Meg Merrilies, and John D. Rockefeller,"[33] but after this second rejection, he told himself that the paper was a failure because Charlotte was "a dull and homespun personage" despite "the éclat of her career."[34] The psychograph itself reveals none of his dissatisfaction, being a well-rounded depiction of a formidable but respectworthy person, with "a solid substructure of New England character," and it has as wonderful a "curtain" as any actress could ask for:

> Yet I confess that I relish most, and even I think Charlotte herself would have relished, the brief epitaph of the Mount Auburn grave-digger, who might have turned up skulls in the cemetery of Elsinore, "She was considerable of a woman, for a play-actress."

The opening of the William Morris Hunt is an excellent summary of Hunt's attitude and importance, from which Bradford proceeds to his characteristics as an artist and as a man. In Section III we return to art, with the emphasis now on "bringing beauty into the hearts and lives of others." The only oddity is a noncommittal weak ending: "Whether he painted great things is beyond my competence to say; but that he loved great things, and lived great things is quite indisputable." Surely there was no more need for such coy modesty here than in the study of any other nonliterary figure.

John Beauchamp Jones, the Confederate or American Pepys, kept a diary in the War Department at Richmond all through the Civil War in which the fortunes of the Confederacy are recorded. Though Bradford gives considerable attention to the character and personality of the diarist, the reader's attention is necessarily divided between him and what he records. Indeed Bradford himself observes that "the element of gathering and constantly increasing tragedy is undoubtedly what obtains most and prevails," and the assassination of Lincoln provides an equally dramatic close for diary and psychograph:

> "It appears that the day of the death of President Lincoln was appointed for illuminations and rejoicings on the surrender of Lee. There is no intelligence of the death of Mr. Seward or his son. It was a dastardly deed—surely the act of a madman."

All in all, "An American Pepys" is a worthy addendum to Bradford's Civil War triliogy.

Chapter Seven

The Psychographs, II

The Watershed: *Damaged Souls* (1923)

Damaged Souls was the work which finally pried Bradford loose from his commitment to the American portrait series. It also caused *Harper's Magazine*, which paid him $300 for each of the psychographs they published—a considerably larger sum than he had received elsewhere—to replace the *Atlantic Monthly*, with which he had been so long identified, as his main magazine outlet, and inspired Harpers and other publishers to make a determined but finally unsuccessful effort to win him away from Houghton Mifflin Company.

It all began with a letter from Lee Foster Hartman, proposing a series of "iconoclastic portraits" for *Harper's Magazine*. To this proposal Bradford replied

that it made "a fascinating appeal to the worst elements of my nature," and that "nothing would amuse me more than to take empty simulacra down from pedestals where they have enjoyed the secure adoration of ages." At the same time I objected that such a work of destruction was not really worth doing, and that in the end it was likely to do more injury to the critic than to the character criticized. I urged that I did not want "to undermine, to overthrow, to destroy even the things that deserve it," and I pointed out that "in every character I have portrayed so far it has been my endeavor to find the good rather than the evil, to set the figure firmly on its common human basis, but at the same time to insist that if the human heart were not worth loving, my work would not be worth doing." After reflecting on the matter, I made the counter-proposition, to do "a group of somewhat discredited figures, and not endeavor in any way to rehabilitate or whitewash, but to bring out their real humanity and show that, after all, they have something of the same strength and weakness as all of us." And I suggested that the series might pass under the title of "Damaged" or "Patched Souls."[1]

The list he sent Hartman on March 19, 1922, comprised Benedict Arnold, Thomas Paine, Aaron Burr, John Randolph of Roanoke, P. T. Barnum, Benjamin F. Butler, Jim Fiske, and Boss Tweed. The last two did not appear in *Damaged Souls* or elsewhere in Bradford, and John Brown was added. Others considered were Poe, Brigham Young, and John Wilkes Booth,

That *Damaged Souls* would be Bradford's best-seller was far from immediately apparent. During its first three months, it sold only 300 copies, including those the author bought himself, thus causing him both to be sure it was mediocre and to flirt with the idea of changing publishers. In June 1923 Mrs. Bradford stopped at the Harper offices in New York to ask if the magazine cared to serialize *The Soul of Samuel Pepys* and to offer the firm book rights if they did; with the usual fierce Bradford honesty, she gave them the sales figures on *Damaged Souls*. But there had been plenty to worry about before any question of sales could arise. There was the tone of the book for one thing, and though Mrs. Bradford somewhat relieved her husband's mind by assuring him he had avoided "being either too solemnly and preachily condemnatory or . . . apparently condonative,"[2] this did not take care of everything. As Bradford wrote one correspondent, he grew very fond of his subjects.

They are all so human, the heroic, wilful Arnold, the quick, kindly, sensitive, generous Burr, the enthusiastic idealist Paine, the sensitive, passionate Randolph, the heroic Brown, the rollicking Barnum, yes, even the sordid but infinitely round good-natured Butler—I love them all, so much that I am ashamed of myself, and begin really to feel that I am only fit to go to hell in their company, whereas, when I get hold of a saint, I immediately begin to pick flaws.[3]

And, as always, there were fluctuations in his estimate of the value of his work. When he finished the Burr, he thought it one of the best things he had done, yet after it had appeared in *Harper's*, he was sure it was such a failure that the editors would never want anything more from him.

The Benjamin F. Butler he regarded so unfavorably that he was inclined to think it ought not to have been published. He put more time and thought into it than in anything else he had done since the Lee and wrote 8,400 words without having made up his mind whether his subject was "a complete scoundrel, or only half a one, or very little of a one." It was "like climbing through barbed entanglements to attempt to get at the fellow's soul."[4] Therefore he tried first summing up what Butler's enemies thought of him, then invoking his friends, and finally permitting him to present his own case. The first two sections, though impressive, are inconclusive, and Section III, which is drawn from *Butler's Book*, even more so, while the last brief section, on Butler's power of expression, is hardly more than an epilogue.

John Randolph presented problems of an entirely different kind. Bradford found him "in some respects the noblest" in his gallery, but all his endowments "were blighted by defects of temper and nerves which made the man's influence for good largely nil." The "eccentric gyrations" of his "perturbed spirit" are followed first in his public activity, then in the private sphere, and the paper closes with a study of the inadequacy of his own inner spiritual resources to nourish the springs of his life. When an historian called the piece harsh, Bradford wrote that he himself had found Randolph "very sympathetic, and was drawn to him by unusual ties of personal experience in many ways."[5] He takes his leave of his subject as "a rich and powerful and much endowed spirit endlessly and uselessly tormenting itself," a man who had many advantages and turned them all to naught because he never learned how to control his own inner world. In his journal, Bradford summed it all up for himself: Randolph's was "a perturbed, wretched, diseased, damaged, interesting soul—like mine."[6]

The author himself pointed out that the first two sections of his John Brown are "plain, bald, chronological narrative" and that, though the last two are more psychographic, "still I have indulged myself far more than usual in the discussion of general principles," using Brown "as a type or model of the fanatical religious temperament" because he was "vastly more interesting as a type than as a man."[7] But though Bradford admits the fanaticism and allows adequately for all its evils and dangers, his judgment of Brown is far more lenient than that of modern historians tends to be, and his letters only make it worse. In 1922 he approved of a project to erect a statue to Brown in Connecticut because of his "magnificent devotion to the highest laws of God, as he understood them, and his readiness to sacrifice life, fortune, and all worldly considerations to carrying out these laws."[8] A little more than a month later, he wrote two different correspondents in terms which many readers today must find as outrageous as anything Thoreau or Sanborn said at the time of Brown's execution: "He was a strange creature, in some ways a maleficent creature; but I am inclined to think the spirit of the Lord was upon him, in spite of the freaks in which it showed itself, as indeed it is apt to do, to our poor human apprehension." And again: "I should regard it as a very bright spot in my genealogical record, if I had the honor to be connected with one of the followers of John Brown."[9]

There is considerable background material also in the Arnold, the Burr, and the Paine, necessitated, especially in the first two instances, by the historic events in which the subjects were involved. The Paine opens and closes with generalizations about rebels and rebellion, ending characteristically with the personal observation that though rebels are "occasionally foul-mouthed and slovenly, and often vain, noisy, and altogether distasteful, they are the power that moves the world. I sometimes wish I had the courage and the character to be a rebel myself." A preliminary judgment of Paine ("he was just a commonplace rebel, entirely practical, a trifle sordid, and altogether English") is entered at the beginning, before any evidence can be adduced to support it, and there is little direct analysis of his character in the first section. But Section II describes his personal characteristics in connection with his work, while Section III deals with his more personal aspects.

The Arnold begins rapidly, orienting the reader, indicating the author's attitude, and noting the complexity of the subject's character. The rest of Section I is devoted to Arnold's "good" qualities, a summary which may not greatly impress those who do not care for the military virtues, and Section II to his faults. Section III probes and seeks to understand the motives behind his treason, and Section IV covers the last, sad years in England. The structure is very formal and expounded explicitly step by step, and the author offers more direct moral judgment than generally.

In spite of the severe judgment of Aaron Burr entered in his portrait of Theodosia, this rascal would seem to have been almost as much Bradford's weakness as hers; he wrote Hartman while working on his portrait of Burr that the task had "gone far to indemnify me for a strictly virtuous life," and he confided to his journal that he could not think when he had had "such a delightful companion, so totally different from anything I am myself, and in many respects what I should like to be, only that it is inconceivable I should be."[10] He meets the lechery head on (Burr came into the world to amuse himself through enjoying women and dominating men), giving no details of Burr's transgressions, but classifying him carefully: he was not "a melancholy, world-weary lover" nor "a self-devouring romantic lover" nor yet "a bitter, cynical lover." "His pleasure in his relations with women was mainly part of the entertainment he derived at all times from the society of his fellow human beings," which provides the connection between Burr's sensuality and his more general human traits and also helps to explain his undeniable charm and, in a measure, even the puzzling adoration of his high-minded daughter. The second part shows him as a trifler in public affairs even as in love. In the last part, there is more analysis of character, differentiated from what has gone before only by the focus being placed upon Burr's later years.

This leaves only the Barnum. Though not all would regard him as a damaged soul, there is little controversial in Bradford's presentation of him as "a trifling bubble of riotous and somewhat vulgar laughter on the stream of the infinite illusion." Section I strikes the keynote of genial showmanship and describes his general qualities of character and temperament. Section II concerns his genius for publicity, and Section III weighs the vast benefaction of his entertainment value against the elements of deceit and vulgarity involved in his exhibitions.

Three European Volumes:
The Soul of Samuel Pepys (1924); *Bare Souls* (1924); *Saints and Sinners* (1932)

The Soul of Samuel Pepys was the first book Bradford had devoted to a single figure since *Lee the American*. It was divided into seven chapters: "The Man and the Diary," "Pepys and His Office," 'Pepys and His Money," "Pepys and Humanity," "Pepys and His Intellect," "Pepys and His Wife," and "Pepys and God." If this is compared with the chapter headings in *Lee the American*, the advance in integration and consequent mastery of psychographic structure will be evident.

Long an admirer of what is by common consent the greatest of all English diaries, Bradford had offered Bliss Perry an article on "The Diary of Pepys as Literature" for the *Atlantic* as early as 1904, and in the summer of 1922 he came close to outlining the book we have in a letter to a friend. Both Harpers and Alfred Harcourt wanted it, and at one time it was planned that *Harper's Magazine* should print at least four chapters (for which portions of *Bare Souls* were later substituted) and that Harper & Brothers should publish both the Pepys and the two succeeding books. But when Houghton Mifflin's sale of *Damaged Souls* turned out to be much larger than Bradford had expected, Harpers agreed to relinquish the Pepys on condition that they might retain *Bare Souls* and *Wives*. In June 1923 Bradford wrote the *Harper's* editor Lee Foster Hartman that "always before, if I may say so without boasting, I have felt as if

I could write on a level with my quotations; but this time I am beaten, and my setting seems poor and plain enough beside the jewels it contains."[11] A month later, however, the book strikes him as "the most racy, piquant vivacious thing I have ever done."[12]

He sees Pepys as a very able man and a worthy public servant, honest at least by the standards of his time, an average man in character but much more than that in his ability to reveal it, and far above the average in his passion for books and music. Since Bradford had already written of Mrs. Pepys in *Portraits of Women*, he had to be careful to avoid repetition when he came to the chapter on domestic life. He presents the lady sympathetically, making a valiant effort to recover her own point of view wherever it can be ascertained. All in all, this is a delightfully human chapter, with just enough spice supplied by the husband's occasional brutality, oddly and inconsistently intermingled with his consideration, and by the incurable infidelities in which he engaged. The subject being what he was, the closing chapter on religion is surprisingly rich and varied and develops many unexpected angles, and the masterly and characteristic closing paragraph shows that the author himself was fully aware of this:

Perhaps it will be thought that, in discussing a busy, active, external, material life, I am giving too much weight to God altogether. It is because the vast, brooding consciousness of God alone gives such a life all its significance—and all its emptiness, and because I believe the busy, active, external, material life of America to-day, so much the life personified by the great Diarist, needs God more than anything else to save it. How the need is to be satisfied is another question and one that can never be answered from the Diary of Pepys.[13]

The subjects in *Bare Souls* are Voltaire, Thomas Gray, Horace Walpole, William Cowper, Charles Lamb, John Keats, Gustave Flaubert, and Edward Fitzgerald, and the materials are almost wholly drawn from their correspondence. The title comes from Sainte-Beuve: "All at once the surface of life is torn apart, and we read bare soul."[14]

These men were all writers, and one may well say all were bachelors, for only Fitzgerald ever led a woman to the altar and he hardly kept her long enough to count. For all that, there is no lack of variety in these pages. Voltaire was preeminently a creature of superb spiritual vitality ("I have never been able to understand how anybody could be cold; that is too much for me"), Walpole essentially a dilettante. The "whole purpose" of Flaubert's existence was "to interpret life in beautiful words." "Though Keats burned out his life at twenty-five, consumed by the passion for creating great poetry, he was no visionary, no crack-brained dreamer, but a sane, sound, normal human being, as Shakespeare was." Gray's life was set in solitude; he "supported himself with decency and dignity, lived long in his remote, sequestered corner and melted out of the world, apparently, as a man, a perfect bit of alms for the vast erasure of oblivion." Charles Lamb was "a creature of whim and frolic fancy, turned life upside down and inside out, sported with it, trifled with it, tossed it in the air like soap bubbles or thistledown, regardless of where it fell or whom it might light upon," a fact which gave Bradford an excellent opportunity to compare him to the Elizabethan or Shakespearean Fools he loved so much. But he does not suppress the tragedy of madness in the Lamb family, which, though it reached its height in Charles's sister Mary, did not leave him totally unscathed.

The study of Keats is notable for both its passionate response to Keats as a poet and for the complete sympathy with which it portrays his love for Fanny Brawne. For Fanny herself, however, the author displays no such admiration as Amy Lowell manifested in her massive biography of Keats. On Fanny's remark after her lover's death—"The kindest act would be to let him rest forever in the obscurity to which circumstances have condemned him"—Bradford makes one of his very sharpest comments—"A human being does not often have a chance to damn himself more completely than that" —yet her statement reveals nothing worse than a failure properly to understand the value of Keats's poetry, which, in her circumstances and at that time, was surely not a crime. But Bradford is at his best

in his reply to those who were shocked by Keats's love letters and
thought they should never have been published:

To me this is quite incomprehensible. Keats's passion is as much a part
of him as his genius. He was thoroughly human, his passion was
thoroughly human, and the force with which it seized him was too
thoroughly human to be in any way degrading. The agonies of fantastic
jealousy, the torments and longings of absence and despair—who that
has really loved will misinterpret them or feel that they disfigure genius
and disgrace it?

Yet he feels that the poet's early death may not have been an un-
mitigated calamity:

He went believing in the endless possibility of love, the endless possibility of beauty, without finding as so many do that love satiates and
beauty fades. It is true that he was not sure of his future fame; but
would he have been more sure at eighty? Who ever is? And the thought
of what he lost is less than of what he escaped.

And the psychograph closes with a beautifully described memory
of the poet's grave at Rome and an unidentified quotation from one
of Bradford's own poems.

But the masterpiece in *Bare Souls* is the portrait of Cowper.
Bradford never did a finer piece of work, and it may well be
doubted that any other writer ever surpassed it in kind. The basis
for the study of Cowper is hell, for the man lived all his later life
under the shadow of the conviction that, since he had committed
the unpardonable sin, hell must be his eternal home. That fact the
reader must never be permitted to forget, for Cowper never forgot
it. Once when he was crossing a cemetery at night, a gravedigger
accidentally struck him with a skull. "The incident impressed him
deeply, and skulls were hitting him from somewhere all his life."
When he was dying, a friend tried to convince him that God's
mercy could embrace even him, but "up to the very end he preferred being damned to being convinced."

Yet hell must not be overemphasized in a portrait of Cowper or the result will be a caricature. It permeated a life filled otherwise with personal charm, love of nature, tenderness toward animals, charity, interest in people, in art, and in music, and all these things must somehow find their place. You think of him with Mrs. Unwin "in that cozy, drowsy atmosphere of English fireside routine. Women petted him, cats purred about him, he held endless skeins of worsted, cracked his little pleasant jokes, drank oceans of tea. And all the time within an inch of his foot opened that black, unfathomable gulf of hell."

Gray and Fitzgerald seem less vivid than the other persons in this volume and Walpole considerably less vital. The keynote of Fitzgerald's portrait—idleness—is, after all, a negative thing. "He walked a little, talked a little, thought a little, scribbled a little as he would have said himself, smoked a great deal, and died"; indeed Bradford devotes a whole section to considering what he might have done had he chosen to do anything. Nevertheless, both Fitzgerald and Gray wrote many wonderful letters, and it must have been a challenge to try to make them interesting enough to find a place between the same set of covers as Voltaire and Keats.

Walpole of course was as busy as a bee, and he reflects as much of the eighteenth century as any man could who chose to live so much on the surface of life. The last section of the portrait, a rather extended account of the somewhat embarrassing passion which the blind, aging Madame du Deffand cherished for him, strikes a deeper note, and the whirligig of time brought in his revenges when he himself was smitten, though less desperately, with the lovely young Berry sisters; certainly Bradford's final judgment on his life and indifferentism is devastating: "it is a damnable reflection upon life, personal life, your life and my life, that the best thing to do with it is to forget it."

Flaubert is another matter altogether, for no writer ever devoted himself to literature with greater ardor and devotion. Even here, however, reservations enter. Though Flaubert was far from inhuman, "his art was his life, and the rest was mere distraction," and even if we wish to make an exception of his love for Louise Colet, we shall still be forced to conclude that "he was a singular lover." Nevertheless, though "*Madame Bovary* is the triumph of the art, . . . the letters are the triumph of the artist."

It is interesting to note that *The Soul of Samuel Pepys* and *Bare Souls* were both written between April and December 1923.

Saints and Sinners appeared when Bradford was on his death-bed; when it arrived, he tried to write his name in his wife's copy but was too weak to finish the signature. On the assumption that three saints ought to be able to balance four sinners, it covers "The Riot of Youth: Caesar Borgia," "God's Vagabond: Saint Francis of Assisi," "The Devil's Vagabond: Casanova," "Alone with God: Thomas à Kempis," "The Prince of Darkness: Talleyrand," "God and the World: Fénelon," and "The Glory of Sin: Byron."[15]

Caesar Borgia gave the most trouble, for Bradford had hardly a word of the subject's own to go upon, "only intangible and unreliable gossip and an almost impenetrable cloud of myth and scandal."[16] If possible, there was even less personal information available about Thomas à Kempis, reputed author of *The Imitation of Christ*, and, for other reasons, at one time Bradford even had quite unnecessary doubts about the Byron. "The first half, depicting the character directly from the prose is excellent, I am sure. But the remainder, filling out the lights and shades with richer and more splendid color from the poetry, is more experimental and may wholly fail."[17] Dale Warren suggested that Gandhi and Harding be used in place of Fénelon and Byron. Bradford mentioned this to *Harper's* after they had rejected the Saint Francis ("Saint Francis is a jewel if I do say it"),[18] and he himself thought of Oscar Wilde as another possible substitute for Byron, but neither he nor Fénelon were ever displaced, and Bradford wept over the last page of the Fénelon after he had finished it. One of the most interesting and amusing dialogues in Bradford's "Journal" is the one he wrote between Warren and Ferris Greenslet discussing *Saints and Sinners*. Though Greenslet thinks that as a whole it is as good as anything Bradford has done, he feels some doubt about the Casanova; "a more natural sinner might have done it better." Yet he judges the book as a whole "brilliant" and "showy" and finds many touches in it of which Strachey would not need to feel ashamed.[19]

Bradford was not able to get serial publication for any of the papers in *Saints and Sinners* except in the *Catholic World* (Thomas à Kempis) and the *South Atlantic Quarterly* (Saint Francis and Talleyrand). Sedgwick, equally indifferent to vice and virtue, would read neither the Saint Francis nor the Caesar Borgia, and *Harper's*, after yammering for months about how much they wanted the Casanova, which they planned to run under the cheap, journalistic heading, "A New Englander Looks at Casanova," rejected it when it finally came to them. All this shows much about the magazines but nothing about the book, for it is one of Bradford's very best and shows him, at sixty-nine, at the height of his powers, capable of making the saints quite as vivid as the sinners.

Caesar Borgia represents the Renaissance physical man, bent on "glory through conquest and cruelty," while Talleyrand, the indifferent skeptic who "accumulated money by crooked means," was so different from him that about the only thing Bradford can give him credit for, aside from his social charm, is the love of peace, or at least hatred of war, which made him a brake upon Napoleon.

The two predominantly sexual sinners, Casanova and Byron, could not well have been more unlike each other either. Casanova, the wanderer, adventurer, idler, and charlatan, who got his money by gambling and "projects" and was always as ready to give as to grasp, "kept up a sexual revel for the endless varied delight of it, without a moment of compunction or remorse." To the Puritan Byron, who used sin as an avenue to glory, or at least a means of attracting attention, "the remorse was the stamp of sin, without which the whole exhibition would have been worthless." He was not in the least like Pepys, "who sinned against his will and suffered the pricks of conscience afterwards, real pricks. To Byron the pricks were theoretical, like the sin, and both made gorgeous material to flaunt before a gasping world." The study of Casanova is, on the whole, denigrating; Bradford finds that Casanova had little to say and has difficulty crediting the man's veracity. He finds vulgarity in Byron, too, "the wayward, mischievous, malignant child," and quotes with approval Goethe's judgment: *"Sobald er reflectiert, ist er ein Kind."* Yet the portrait of Byron is drenched in the same glamour that informs his poetry, and its creator's failure to perceive this is one of his most glaring misjudgments of his own work.

Distressed by the indifference of the magazine editors to *Saints and Sinners*, Bradford wrote his friend and disciple Ambrose White Vernon:

> They want the immediate present, Sedgwick especially, though I have labored to convince him that I am working in the immediate present all the time and my one object in resurrecting all these ghostly figures of the past is the better understanding and interpretation of the hopes and passions and struggles of today. This Sedgwick does not seem to grasp, nor do the Harper people do very much better. Yet I think I shall not give in to them, but shall go my own road and try to convince them that if they want to understand the men and women about them, they have got to look into the souls of the men and women of an earlier day.[20]

As an abstract proposition, this is incontrovertible, but Bradford rather overemphasizes it in trying to establish relevancies. As in *Daughters of Eve* he had presented Ninon de Lenclos as "just such a girl as New York breeds to-day by dozens," so in the Borgia portrait he labors resemblances between the Renaissance and the modern spirit, especially in connection with "the joyous youth of today [which] proclaims the sacred right to indulge its instincts without trammel or restraint." In a letter to Frederick L. Allen of *Harper's*, he went so far as to claim that the piece "comes pretty close to the young life of today."[21] But whatever one may think of our young sexual emancipates, certainly there is no more reason for attributing an inclination to Borgia-like crimes to them than to their elders. In his study of Saint Francis, on the other hand, Bradford makes much of the, this time, perfectly valid contrast between the modern spirit and the Franciscan poverty, chastity, and obedience.

Though Bradford once said that Saint Francis was too close to insanity easily to come to terms with, nobody could have made "God's Vagabond" more winning than he made him. It is true that, even here, he is characteristically impressed by the inability of even the saints to achieve complete unselfishness ("the day will come," Francis is quoted as having said, "when I shall be adored by the whole world"). Yet the great thing about this saint is that, despite all his excesses, he never lost sight of the fact that though "he wanted to make over the world, . . . he wanted to make it over by love, and love does not destroy." And, for all the antipathy between modern freedom and medieval asceticism, it is this portrait which contains the most directly autobiographical passage in all Bradford's psychographs, the account of how, when he was engaged to be married, he and his love were tempted to set up their lives on the basis of something like a Franciscan poverty, and how, though they yielded at last to pressure from their elders, "there are times when I wish I had behaved as Francis did."

Naturally we do not see Thomas à Kempis with anything like the clarity that obtains with Saint Francis. Much of the first section is devoted to a description of the monastic life and consideration of whether Thomas really was the author of the *Imitation*. Nevertheless the analysis of the praise of solitude, negation of self, and complete subjection to the will of God is masterly, as is the closing section on "the extraordinary qualities of literary beauty, which make the *Imitation* one of the masterpieces of the world." Who but Bradford could have dreamed of writing, "The Daphnis and Chloë of Longus is a monument of Pagan naturalism, but the delicate rippling cadences of the Greek and the simple human touch all through the book often remind one of the *Imitation*"?

The complicated and sophisticated François de Salignac de la Mothe Fénelon, an aristocrat, a gentleman, an aspiring statesman, almost an exquisite, a lover of literature and art, and himself the author of a French educational classic, seems far removed from the heavenly simplicities of Thomas and Francis, yet his saintly character is clearly established, and Bradford might well have extended his admiration for the last page of his psychograph to the whole closing section, for it is a masterly analysis of religious feeling, as manifested by Fénelon in his final phase. Incidentally, one of Bradford's most astonishing personal statements is that Fénelon and Talleyrand were the two subjects in *Saints and Sinners* that he found most congenial because they were most like himself![22]

A Trilogy of Faith and Doubt:
D. L. Moody, A Worker in Souls (1927); *Darwin* (1926); *Life and I: An Autobiography of Humanity* (1928)

"I am getting extraordinarily interested in doing a sort of trilogy," wrote Bradford in 1925, "the Moody first, rather representing the Fundamentalist point of view, then the Darwin for the other side, then a study of Christ to crown the whole."[23] Though both the Moody and the Darwin are psychographs, they involve more elaborate ideational backgrounds than any other of Bradford's works, and *Life and I* is not a psychograph at all unless it is a psychograph of humankind. Because of its intimate relationship to the other books, it must, however, be considered here.

It all began on March 11, 1925, when John Farrar wrote, asking Bradford to do a book about the evangelist Moody, to be serialized in the *Ladies' Home Journal* and published by George H. Doran. Immediately fired with enthusiasm, Bradford outlined the whole work in his mind and began writing without even waiting for publishing arrangements to be completed. To be sure, he foresaw difficulties. He had associations with the Moody schools at Northfield, where his beloved sister-in-law, Harriet Ford Cutler, to whose memory he dedicated his work without being at all sure she would have approved of it, had been a teacher; on the other hand, he feared the modernists might well join the agnostics and the secularists in feeling that the evangelist had been presented too sympathetically.[24] But as the work progressed, he became more and more absorbed in it. He found he did not need to do much studying, for "all the philosophical reading and thinking I had done in the past . . . seemed to come into play, and to supply me with ideas for more than I could possibly use within the limits I had set myself."[25] "Never, never," he confided to his journal, "have I so completely poured out my full heart, never put all my soul, all my passion, all my question, all my despair so abundantly into a book as I have and shall into this."[26] He did worry lest the rich background might swamp the central figure, and the passion he poured into his writing must have involved considerable strain. "There are times when my attitude toward Moody is wholly murderous [he was, as usual, reading detective stories at night], and again times when the inimitable humor and pathos overcome me to a sympathetic smile, and again times when I wonder whether I had not better be busy about saving my own soul, he makes hell glare with such a tormenting efflorescence."[27] But he finished the book six months to a day from the time he received Farrar's letter.

The real difficulty, however, came from the way the *Journal* and its editor, Barton W. Currie, dragged their feet. At one time Bradford thought the whole deal was off, but he salvaged it by offering to write the chapter on Moody and Sankey on approval; if Currie turned it down, the project would be scrapped; if he liked it, the author would go on to Chapters 1 and 2, and the final decision made then. Currie himself found the material absorbingly interesting, but he evidently developed serious doubts about its appeal to his readers, for though he paid the author $7,500, he delayed long before he printed it, inconspicuously and badly cut, "castrated," said Bradford, with "everything that remotely suggested brains" having been eliminated.[28] Thus, though written before the Darwin, the Moody was not published until after it. Ironically, *McCall's* made a bid for it just after Bradford had committed himself to the *Journal*. Through the agent Ann Watkins, Bradford then tried to interest them and other popular magazines in the Darwin (the *Delineator*, too, was flirting with him at the time, and he thought it would be piquant if the Darwin might run there while the Moody was appearing in the *Journal*), but the editors of all the mass circulation magazines shied from Darwin for fear of offending their Fundamentalist readers. Harpers and Harcourt were both interested in the books, but the Moody stayed with Doran, who had commissioned it, and the Darwin went to Houghton Mifflin, who rewarded Bradford with the best contract they had given him yet. The most sensational chapter, "The Destroyer," was also published in *Harper's Magazine*.

D. L. Moody, A Worker in Souls comprises seven chapters: "The Growth of a Soul," "Heaven and Hell," "Moody the Preacher," "Moody and Sankey," "Moody the Man," "Moody the Man of Business," and "The Molder of Souls." The most psychographic chapters are the last three, especially Chapter 5, which covers systematically Moody's physique, family life, use of money, social relations, and attitude toward art and public affairs; if Bradford had written a short psychograph of Moody, it would have been more like this than any other chapter. Chapter 6 is less specialized than its title might suggest, for it deals not only with business in the narrower sense but with all Moody's association with and management of men.

The least psychographic chapter and the one most definitely focused upon ideas is Chapter 2, which expounds Moody's Gospel—what he believed and taught—against the historic background of Christian, or at least Fundamentalist Protestant, faith, with a whole section on religious revivals before Moody. But this is not the only chapter which contains such background materials. Chapter 1 includes a discussion of conversion phenomena. Chapter 3, on Moody's sermons, has a digression on the power of words. The last chapter, whose main theme is how Moody handled his converts, contains a study of how others have done the same thing, down through the Christian centuries. Chapter 4, on Moody's use of music (which is interesting especially because it is so difficult to understand how a man who was tone-deaf could have had such an uncanny understanding of how music could affect others) embraces not only a short psychograph of his musical collaborator, Ira D. Sankey, but a discussion of music in general, both sacred and secular, and of the author's personal experience with it.

Many comparisons and contrasts are drawn between Moody and other, mainly nineteenth-century, figures, including Lincoln, Grant, Darwin, Sainte-Beuve, and Barnum; the Shakespearean Fool bobs up from time to time as a kind of Moody antitype. "I wish to keep him, like a gleaming thread running through all these various chapters,"[29] says Bradford; he is very frank about outlining the book before the reader's eyes. But psychography is never forgotten; even Chapter 1, which is organized chronologically, covering Moody's life to his departure from Chicago, rests its emphasis upon his human characteristics, as developed through the circumstances of his early life.

If Moody reminded Bradford of Charles Darwin, it must have been because they were so different, for, as the biographer saw it, Darwin's evolutionary philosophy made Moody's conception of religion impossible for many people. Though Bradford himself was one of these, he regarded it as a great loss, and the chapter on "The Destroyer" traces the blighting effect of Darwinism in many fields and avenues of human thought and experience. The poignancy of the contrast was greatly deepened by the character of the man who brought it about. In 1921 Bradford wrote a friend:

Of all the men who made the glory of the nineteenth century I do not think any single one comes so near my heart as Charles Darwin, not in his scientific speculations, but in his spirit and mental attitude. . . . Never was there any one who so thoroughly combined intense earnestness, the faculty of enormous labor, with largeness and sweetness of soul, infinite candor and tolerance, broad comprehension of the position and arguments of others, instant readiness to abandon the conclusions and theories of a life-time, if necessary, out of pure, humble deference to the revelation of truth.[30]

The next year he wrote even more directly and feelingly:

I regard him, with Longfellow, whom in so many ways he resembles, as one of the finest, noblest types that any age has produced. Patience, tolerance, gentleness, kindness, simplicity, loyalty to an ideal—if these are not Christian virtues, what are?[31]

Like the Moody, the Darwin contains seven chapters: "The Observer," "The Thinker," "The Discoverer," "The Loser," "The Lover," "The Destroyer," and "The Scientific Spirit."

The first chapter opens biographically, then proceeds to the consideration of the faculty of observation in human beings in general and in various specific types and examples. The second division of the chapter confines itself to Darwin's own habits and characteristics as an observer, but there are many general considerations again in Sections III and IV. Observation, though indispensable, does not get us far without thought ("Knowledge is the accumulation of facts. Wisdom is the establishment of relations");[32] hence "The Observer" must be followed by "The Thinker," which explores Darwin's methods and processes, establishes his limitations, and describes his attitudes in this area, again, as in the Moody, employing comparisons and contrasts with other figures. We are now ready, in Chapter 3, to "take up the supreme interest of Darwin's life, the dramatic study of the conception, elaboration, promulgation, and triumph of his evolutionary theory." Scientifically considered, these first three chapters are the most solid in the book and would have been the "toughest" to serialize. Bradford never ceased to be concerned with his own lack of scientific training but comforted himself by remembering that his concern was not with the theories themselves but the man who held them.

"The Loser" and "The Lover" are pure psychography. The first concerns what Darwin himself recognized and lamented as the gradual shrinking of his life interests to scientific matters.

My mind seems to have become a kind of machine for grinding general laws out of large collections of facts, but why this should have caused the atrophy of that part of the brain alone, on which the higher tastes depend, I cannot conceive. A man with a mind more highly organized or better constituted than mine, would not, I suppose, have thus suffered, and if I had to live my life again, I would have made a rule to read some poetry or listen to some music at least once every week; for perhaps the parts of my brain now atropied would thus have been kept active through use.

He added that "now for many years I cannot endure to read a line of poetry: I have tried lately to read Shakespeare, and found it so intolerably dull that it nauseated me." He did better with music, and the novel furnished at least a partial exception to his indifference to literature, but even nature inspired no rapture in the sense in which the Romantic poets understood it. Nor did politics interest him much more, except when, as in the case of the American Civil War, his hatred of slavery caused him to become a partisan. Finally, though he was never hostile to religion, he was largely indifferent to it, and "it does not appear that he felt the need and the longing and the desire that torture some of us." But "if Darwin was not conspicuous as a lover of God, he was at least notable in every way as one who loved his fellow men." In the chapter on "The Lover" this is developed in general and with special reference to his exceptionally happy family life, though it is interesting that "even when he was engaged, his love for Emma Wedgwood does not seem to have been of the kind that stings and burns." Darwin's invalidism and the problems it occasioned naturally gave Bradford a strong fellow feeling for him in his personal and domestic aspects.

There is less psychography in the last two chapters. "The Destroyer" ponders the paradox of Darwin, "the gentle, the kindly, the human, who could not bear the sight of blood, who raged against the cruelty of vivisection and slavery, who detested suffering in men and animals" coming at last to typify "the vigorous logic that wrecked the universe for me and for millions of others." In the blurb material he supplied his publishers, Bradford wrote of Darwin that he made hell a laughing-stock and heaven a dream, with God Himself left as no more than an amiable possibility, and though he was not pleased when they featured this statement on what he regarded as an oversensational jacket, they can hardly be accused of misrepresenting his book. He knew that many thinkers and common folk alike had found the evolutionary hypothesis quite compatible with both theistic belief and an optimistic outlook, and his discussion shows a reasonable familiarity with their views, but after having begun his chapter with an account of Darwin's own attitude toward the religious implications of his theory, he turns to his own impression of the results of the popular acceptance of Darwinism and finds them devastating. Though he grants that since "mankind has always demanded spiritual ideas and the divine presence, and always will demand them," reinventing them when lost and re-creating them when destroyed, it seems probable that some read-justment will be made, it is clear that neither William James nor John Fiske nor anybody else has helped him personally to make it. The depressing tone of the "Destroyer" chapter is counteracted to a certain extent by the final chapter on "The Scientific Spirit," as exemplified primarily in Darwin himself. Bradford argues that "the scientific qualities develop into virtues to some extent akin to the Christian ideal—humility, tolerance, self-abnegation, and devotion to truth." But even though "universal scepticism surely carries with it the privilege of universal hope," yet "for the mass of mankind assuredly the scientific spirit and the pure pursuit of truth are not enough."

Bradford conceived *Life and I*, full-fledged, before he had even finished the Moody. It was first supposed to be called "Christ and I," but nearly all his advisers said no. In January 1927, Ferris Greenslet definitely rejected "Christ and I," suggesting the present title; then, in October, he reopened the question, but both Brad-ford's wife and daughter were strongly opposed, and by now he too had his doubts. "Christ and I" really meant "Christ and the I," that is, the human ego, and at one point Bradford pondered "Christ and the Capital I," with an epigraph from Moody: "Oh, if we could keep down this capital I, and keep Christ up."[33] In a sense, *Life and I* is also a misleading title, especially without the subtitle *An Autobiography of Humanity*, which did not appear on the cover, for it suggests that the book is more limited and personal than it is.

Bradford wrote the key chapter, "Christ and I," first. Mrs. Brad-ford liked it, though she was sure some readers would be shocked, and her husband had some doubts about going on, but decided to write Chapter 1, "Love and I," anyway. "What will Helen think of this one? What will Greenslet think of the two? What do I think of them myself?"[34] After a month's agonizing delay, Greenslet read the two chapters and wrote enthusiastically, and Bradford finished *Life and I*, after eight weeks of work, on November 20, 1926.

The purpose of the book was "to make a dramatic presentation of the greatest dramatic struggle in the world, that between the I and the Not-I, between the everlastingly aggressive, all-engrossing self and the objects that attract or repel it, the manifold, conflicting forces against which it must assert itself triumphantly, or else tragically and miserably perish." The first four chapters—"Love and I," "Power and I," "Beauty and I," and "Thought and I"—deal with "the most marked phases in which the I asserts itself." The central chapter, "Christ and I," typifies "the greatest agency which has ever been developed for overcoming the I," and the three concluding chapters—"Christ and the Not-I," "Christ and More Than I," and "Christ and I and God"—"show how this and similar agencies have been applied."[35]

Self-propagation is the leading subject of Chapter 1 and self-preservation that of the three chapters which follow. Bradford is quite frank in indicating the power of sexual passion, but he will not assert its complete identity with the body. On its highest level, the sexual act is an expression of "the effort of the I to enlarge or escape itself," a "struggle of bodies to be melted, dissolved, lost in each other, in the desperate effort to blend souls." This is the glory of love and sex; its tragedy is that success can never be more than relative; complete harmony between two human beings is never achieved.

Nor do human beings succeed in escaping from the I in other aspects. We seek association with others because we are attracted to them or curious about them, to cast off loneliness, and because many of our ends cannot be achieved without their cooperation. But we cannot go far without measuring ourselves against them, without desiring to excel or to dominate, most crudely in sports and games, most horribly and destructively in physical combat and war. Influence and power may also be won through persuasion, the accumulation of money, or promotion to a position of power, through business, and even in the home.

The I intrudes even into both the creation and the enjoyment of beauty. The actor and the singer revel in applause, and however sincere the poet and the painter may be in their desire to create and diffuse beauty, they hunger for fame, whether they acknowledge it or not, and the price they pay for achievement is a never-

ending struggle against both external and internal difficulties. "The
career of an artist," said Whistler, "always begins tomorrow."

And thought. We begin by trying to understand the human
beings around us, but we never do, nor, for that matter, ourselves.
From here we pass to larger matters, where the field of investigation
is more inaccessible, culminating in "the metaphysical, which seeks
to probe the nature of man and God, and of thought itself." But
even here "the persistent, unescapable I intrudes." Philosophers are
as ambitious as athletes and may even espouse their theories and
support them because they have a vested interest in them rather
than because they are correct.

Bradford made "Christ and I" his central chapter because he saw
the Christian religion as foremost among "the agencies that do
battle with the I." But much of the chapter is devoted to a study
of the Gospels as the source for knowledge of Jesus, and Bradford's
account of their deficiencies as historic documents is penetrating
for a man who was not a trained New Testament scholar, writing at
a time when New Testament scholarship was much less advanced
than today. Despite all the shortcomings of the records, he finds
"a perennial fountain of spiritual light and refreshment in the dis-
courses attributed to Jesus," as well as a "heavenly sweetness" and
"ineffable, profound, spiritual insight, which without making a
shadow of pretence, seems to go to the bottom of the world," and
this is the point at which *Life and I* comes closest to psychography.

Mrs. Bradford was still correct, however, in finding much in the
chapter by which Christians must be shocked, for her husband
found Jesus not only indifferent toward the larger affairs of the
world but ignorant of them. To combat its evils he had nothing to
suggest but "a simple and innocent communism, which has its
charm as an ideal, but which the experience of nineteen hundred
years has shown to be utterly impracticable." Except for his appreciation of nature, he apparently cared nothing for beauty, art, intellectual curiosity, or truth in the abstract, and Bradford resented
and resisted "to the death" this "close and strict limitation" of
human interests. Though "transfigured by love," his God was
"mainly the anthropomorphic deity of the Jews and the Old Testa-

ment," and he seems to have expected the imminent end of the present world order in terms of the Jewish apocalyptic tradition, about which he was obviously mistaken. Yet, though his prime interest was in "the little world of the Jews," there are "whisperings and glimmerings" of an interest in "a far wider salvation," and, in spite of the apocalypticism, there are luminous sayings like "The kingdom of God is within you" and "Except ye . . . become as little children, ye shall not enter into the kingdom of heaven."

By the "Not-I" Bradford meant "the denial of the immediate I and its indulgences" in the interest of something larger. There can be no doubt that the Christian religion has often demonstrated its power to deliver men and women from every form of sin and, in the saints and martyrs, even to raise them at times above what we think of as human limitations. Yet "the omnipresent I" may survive even in self-denial, as in the pride often taken in humility or "a strange, perverted . . . desire to excel in sin, in order to emphasize repentance."

The penultimate chapter, "Christ and More Than I," deals with the effort to escape from or overcome the I through positive efforts "to increase the joy of others" or "to relieve or to diminish their sorrows," either through direct attempts to relieve suffering or through reform activity, political, sociological, moralistic, or religious. Yet even when such service takes the extreme form of martyrdom, one can never be sure that the I has been rooted out; there is a self-satisfaction involved even in being faithful unto death.

The final chapter, "Christ and I and God," recognizing that "the craving of the I to assert and to escape itself can find no full satisfaction in this life," explores the human hope of seeking it in the world of the spirit. Though God can no longer be satisfyingly conceived of in the old anthropomorphic terms, "the fundamental, essential longing, craving of the I to get out of itself, somehow, somewhere to achieve a larger, fuller, more complete, enduring existence" can never be satisfied except in religious terms. God may be approached through nature, through mystical communion, or through the prayer by which "one's own narrow, personal will" is surrendered "to the larger will by which the universe moves and has its being," and even if this can be achieved only fleetingly and momentarily, it still comprises incomparably the most precious part of our life experience. Even here, however, there is paradox. The I seeks "absorption in the One, in the Unity which is all pervading and final," yet, as Pascal says, "unity and multiplicity, . . . it is an error to exclude either of the two."

Thus, to the end—and what is the end?—the I continues to assert, to worship, to glorify, and to abominate itself, and after all its infinitely weary struggles, and efforts, and despairs, it asks but one thing, illimitable hope, which no power in the universe can altogether deny it.

Toward Contemporaneity:
The Quick and the Dead (1931)

Bradford had always maintained that it was impossible to do psychographs of contemporaries because the necessary information had been neither accumulated nor evaluated, and he did not break this rule until *The Quick and the Dead* appeared—"The Fury of Living: Theodore Roosevelt," "Brains Win and Lose: Woodrow Wilson," "Let There Be Light: Thomas Alva Edison," "The Wheel of Fortune: Henry Ford," "The World as Idea: Nikolai Lenin," "The World as Will: Benito Mussolini," and "The Genius of the Average: Calvin Coolidge."[36] Edison, Ford, Mussolini, and Coolidge were still "quick" when the book appeared.

It began on June 21, 1929, when Ellery Sedgwick, who had been rather cool to Bradford since he had been publishing in *Harper's*, wrote to ask for a portrait of Coolidge. Though the suggestion broke in upon *Saints and Sinners*, Bradford almost at once envisaged a book covering Roosevelt, Wilson, Lenin, Mussolini, Rockefeller, Ford, and Coolidge, proceeding also to sound out Greenslet's interest. In 1930 Edison was substituted for Rockefeller; the "Letter Books" give no indication why.

As the work progressed, the author was more and more taken with the book, though he did not enjoy it as much as *Daughters of Eve*. Still, if *The Quick and the Dead* must lack the piquant charm of the *Daughters*, he comforted himself with the thought that it might have more substance; he also hoped that these contemporary and near contemporary subjects might be worth more to the magazines than what he had done before. By July 1929 he had worked out a plan for the Coolidge but was worrying over whether such inferior materials as he had available could produce a first-class portrait, and September found him still probing "in the murky and unalluring labyrinth of Calvin Coolidge's soul" and threatening to drop his paper into the wastebasket after he had finished it.[37] On September 27 he settled to "the most tremendous and critical piece of work I have attempted for a long time," after which, having had an inoculation, he took to his bed with a fever and did not return to his desk till October 7. On the twelfth he finished the psychograph, feeling that he had "established the humanness of a rather inhuman personage and . . . put in the varied lights and shadows with about as much skill as any would be likely to command on such a subject."[38] Hereupon he wrote Sedgwick that his paper was finished but that he hesitated to send it to him.

You have seemed of late to be so much out with my work, to be so inclined to emphasize the obvious defects and overlook the merits if there are any, that I fear you may reject it like the others. And I am so foolishly over-sensitive that repeated rejection depresses me unduly. Therefore I am wondering whether it would be better not to bother you and to turn it over to some one else. But I wanted you at least to know that I have carried out your suggestion to the best of my ability.[39]

Sedgwick accepted the portrait with enthusiasm and paid Bradford $250, the highest fee he had ever given him.

Though Bradford's portrait is in no sense deliberately unfriendly, it can hardly have pleased Coolidge or any of his warmest admirers. The mere fact that the author finds it necessary to probe the reasons for Coolidge's success shows that he found it puzzling, and the conclusion, that Coolidge is what the average man is or would like to be, is hardly flattering. Like nearly all the studies in *The Quick and the Dead*, this one is divided into a larger number of sections than Bradford generally used, and its most startling passage is that in which, taking his cue from Heine's study of Shakespeare's Cleopatra, he finds the contrast between "the dark, solemn, austere, mysterious, dreary land of Egypt and the gay, frivolous, trifling Parisian harlot who ruled over it" no more striking than the "contrast between the mad, hurrying, chattering, extravagant, self-indulgent harlotry of twentieth-century America and the grave, silent, stern, narrow, uncomprehending New England Puritanism of Calvin Coolidge."

The psychograph of Thomas Edison is considerably more admiring than either the Coolidge or the Henry Ford, though much of it is descriptive rather than evaluative. Edison's aesthetic limitations are admitted freely ("'Evangeline,' Shakespeare as an inventor, and Beethoven's Ninth Symphony make an aesthetic hodgepodge that puzzles me"), and though the whole last section is devoted to religion, this hardly seems very important. What does appeal to Bradford is what he regarded as Edison's fundamental kindliness, not only in its relation to individuals but in his devotion to a work which he regarded as of benefit to mankind—all of which is presented sympathetically though unsentimentally, for Bradford was never the man to conceive salvation in technological terms.

One feels that Bradford was less sure of all these things with Henry Ford. Perhaps Ford's antiintellectualism or some of the reckless pronouncements he made from time to time repelled, or perhaps it was merely that he had too much money or too much power. In any case, Bradford first thought the Ford materials barren and scanty, then found he had much more than he had supposed, and finally pronounced his job "vastly amusing to do" and hoped it would make amusing reading also.[40] The editors of *Harper's*, who had rejected the Edison, greeted the Ford with jubilation and featured it in the magazine. Nevertheless the ending is chilly, even though softened by the writer's charitably identifying himself with what he perceives as Ford's limitations:

With all the millions, with all the powers, with all the successes, with all the knotty problems solved and forgotten, one somehow gets the impression of a man groping, struggling, striving to adjust a universe that is vastly, tragically inadjustable, in short, of a man forever wrestling with life just like you and me.

Though one was quick and the other dead, Mussolini and Lenin had a certain affinity in that both were dictators. After Bradford's death, Mussolini told an American student of Italian culture that he had found Bradford's portrait of him critical but *"simpatico"* and, through her, sent Mrs. Bradford an autographed photograph of himself. One cannot but feel that he must have been easily satisfied, for the study is far from admiring. "The one overwhelming argument in . . . favor [of democracy] is that in a hundred thousand years mankind has not found anything permanently better and certainly not in the arbitrary, monarchical tyranny and despotism of Lenin and Mussolini." In an imaginary dialogue between Mussolini and his great predecessor Cavour,[41] Bradford had the latter condemn il Duce for his destruction of Italian liberty and see only disaster ahead of him. Bradford himself saw the same—though he did not live long enough to find himself justified—and he devoted his last section to speculations about Mussolini's future, an ending which must obviously have been impossible had he not been writing about a living man.

For all that, the Mussolini *is* more sympathetic than the Lenin. Both men were devoted to a cause; both were, in a sense, puritans in their attitude toward distractions and indulgences; both used human beings unscrupulously to achieve their ends. But Mussolini was decidedly the more "human" of the two (there was something boyish not only in his strutting but in his relish of power), and his emotional range was wider. One need not impugn Lenin's sincerity to see him operating with something resembling the regularity and rigidity of a machine; indeed love of children and of cats is about the only endearing trait Bradford could find in him. How suggestive is his fear of music: "I cannot often let myself listen to music; it acts on my nerves, makes me feel like talking foolishly and caressing the human beings who, living in hell, can create such beauty. Now, as things are to-day, you can't stop to caress people; they would bite your fingers off. You have got to hit heads right and left, to hit them pitilessly, though in the ideal, we are opposed to violence." And surely the famous laughter, whose full significance Bradford admitted he was not able to fathom, was more sinister than genial.

Bradford started his work on Theodore Roosevelt realizing that he had inherited a certain prejudice against him from his father. His first surprise was finding *The Winning of the West* so good— "careful, trained, conscientious scholarship" and "literary craft of a decidedly distinguished order."[42] It seemed "the most enormous task I [have] ever undertaken" to do justice to so many-sided a man, and he wondered whether it might not be better to use the essay on "Biography and the Human Heart" in *The Quick and the Dead* and let the book go with six psychographs instead of seven.[43] Like so many who have written about Roosevelt, Bradford felt humbled in the presence of his subject. "It seems too absurd for such a pigmy as myself to attempt to deal with such a creature, one so puny and frail as I am, physically and spiritually also, one so fluid, so impersistent, so incapable of fixity or solidity or any of the magnificent aspects of character on which Roosevelt prided himself." He remembered that he had felt a similar inferiority toward his father but comforted himself that he had also "cherished a sense of inward superiority" and hoped he might do the same toward T.R. The great man "lived far too much externally, did not turn inward into himself."[44] But Frederick L. Allen made the portrait the leading article in *Harper's* and did not see how it could be much better.

"I do not take to Wilson, I am sorry to say"; thus Bradford in July, 1930.[45] Early in August, not liking him any better, he yet felt that "on the whole he was a bigger man than Roosevelt."[46] He began writing on September 13, for once without a previously formulated outline, but by the fifteenth he had it, and three days later he was rejoicing in more abundant, magnificent material than he had had for T.R. By the end of the month, he felt that though he had not made Wilson very attractive, the psychograph would still be the most powerful thing in his book, but on October 9,

Harper's, whose functionings were nothing if not erratic, turned it down on the ground that neither the subject nor the treatment were very interesting. Oddly enough, Bradford laid himself open to and received another rejection by sending it next to Mencken, before it went to Sedgwick, who liked it immensely and made it his leading article. Writing to Willis H. Abbot, Bradford summed up his attitude toward both Wilson and his great antitype:

Somehow Roosevelt, with all his brilliancy and versatility, seemed like an impulsive boy, yet I could not help loving him, though I started with rather a prejudice the other way. Wilson was far more puzzling, more intricate, more full of strange shades and complicated, subtle corners, yet I did not get to like him, liked him perhaps less when I got through than when I began.[47]

Whether or not they are wholly just, the Roosevelt and Wilson portraits are certainly the most brilliant in *The Quick and the Dead*, and among the author's very best. There are a few misstatements of fact in the Roosevelt: Mrs. Roosevelt did not have considerable property of her own, and we know now that it is far from true that being in love never took hold of Roosevelt "as a devastating spiritual experience." Though there is no clear evidence that Roosevelt had a settled or assured faith in human immortality, it is a gross exaggeration to say that he had no religion and no need of God "because he really had no need of anything save his own immensely sufficient self"; Bradford was so sure of this that he referred to it again in his portrait of Caesar Borgia, where he achieves one of the strangest comparisons of human beings on record when he writes that religion meant no more to Borgia than it did to Lenin or Roosevelt! Nevertheless the psychograph as a whole has the vitality, the bursting energy, and, yes, the charm of its subject.

Both Colonel House and Professor Dodd thought very highly of Bradford's study of Wilson,[48] but it may still be argued that the emphasis upon the man of brains is somewhat overdone. The first paragraph ends on an ominous note: "For brains can do the greatest things in the world, they can develop ideals, they can build up states and civilizations, but they can mislead and ruin and shatter an individual who puts a blind trust in them." The biographical paragraph goes on to tell us that Wilson "died of a brain disease," surely a questionable diagnosis, and the paper ends with a loaded comment on a statement in which Wilson had allowed himself to say, "I know": "He knew, he knew, he always knew, for he was a creature of brains."

Bradford analyzes Wilson's own attitude toward brains in general, from which he proceeds to the qualities of Wilson's own mind, and is excellent in defining limitations. From here he proceeds to the subject's emotional life, finding the intellect dominant even in love and religion; Wilson's "I want people to love me" inspires the comment that all his emphasis is on being loved rather than loving. Bradford's decency and generosity are shown attractively in his rejection of the scandal that some contemporaries tried to read into Wilson's correspondence with Mrs. Peck and others and in his rejection of Roosevelt's characterization of Wilson as a man without ideas or ideals as "merely ridiculous." The psychograph closes with a study of Wilson's motivations and of the effect of his temperament upon his conduct in public life. Agree or disagree with Bradford's judgments, his psychograph of Wilson is still a brilliant, dispassionate analysis, based not upon preconceptions but on one man's honest analysis of the evidence before him.

Addenda: *Portraits and Personalities* (1933); *The Haunted Biographer: Dialogues of the Dead* (1927)

A book of biographical studies for school use was suggested to Bradford by D. C. Heath & Company in 1931, and his first idea was to do fifteen papers of 4,000 words each on Julius Caesar, Napoleon, Washington, Lincoln, Lee, Theodore Roosevelt, Shakespeare, Scott, Mark Twain, Darwin, Florence Nightingale, Edison, Henry Ford, Richard E. Byrd, and Jane Addams. The Heath editor F. W. Scott liked the Shakespeare and the Napoleon, which were completed first, but thought more incident, as well as identification and definition of references, needed for the adolescent reader. After receiving

Scott's letter, Bradford first thought he had better give up the enterprise, then suggested having a writer more familiar with the educational field make the necessary changes and additions. A few days later, he decided not to continue but wondered whether perhaps the six sketches already completed—Washington, Lincoln, Napoleon, Roosevelt, Shakespeare, and Florence Nightingale—might be published alone as "Lives Worth Living."[49] Three months later, the possibility of serial publication in the *Scholastic* or *St. Nicholas* having been raised, he found himself getting interested again. "Lives Worth Living" was not published, however, and *Portraits and Personalities* did not appear until 1933, when Houghton Mifflin brought it out in an educational edition, prepared by Mabel A. Bessey, of the Bay Ridge High School, Brooklyn. To the aforementioned six pieces were added studies of Benedict Arnold, Joseph Jefferson, Louisa May Alcott, Emily Dickinson, and Mark Twain, somewhat shortened, presumably by Miss Bessey, from Bradford's other books, a biographical sketch of Bradford himself, and considerable material for classroom use.[50]

The new material in *Portraits and Personalities* calls for no particular discussion; the sketches represent Bradford's principal attempt to organize his materials in the conventional biographical, rather than psychographic, pattern. In this connection, the Roosevelt is especially interesting as his own only recasting of a psychograph in biographical style. The Shakespeare, simple as it is, reflects wide knowledge as well as enthusiasm; it seems strange that, in spite of his lifelong adoration of Shakespeare ("Ah! how that Shakespeare says everything!"),[51] Bradford should have written of him at any length only here. Aside from being biographical sketches rather than psychographs, the principal difference between the new material in *Portraits and Personalities* and Bradford's other books is that here the approach is less critical. Perhaps the Florence Nightingale comes as close to being an idealized account as anything he ever did, though even here he admits that "no one will deny that even in Florence Nightingale the ego was there." He refers in passing to Washington's "long-continued and, for those days, passionately intimate correspondence with Sally Fairfax [as] but one among his many love affairs," but the closest he comes to questioning the basic rightness of either Washington or Lincoln is his noting that "there are people today who feel that Douglas took the larger view . . . and that Lincoln did not recognize sufficiently the bearing of other economic issues that were quite as significant as slavery."

The "haunted biographer" material, an offshoot of Bradford's psychography, consists of dialogues between various persons of whom Bradford wrote or in whom he was interested. He included characters drawn from his creative as well as his psychographic writing, himself, his publishers and editors, friends and critics. Often the others talk about him, sometimes praising him, more often expressing their dissatisfaction in what he wrote about them. The only publication of these dialogues between covers was in the pamphlet series called University of Washington Chapbooks, *The Haunted Biographer: Dialogues of the Dead* (1927); in it there are three groups, organized around Lincoln, Darwin, and Moody. Three briefer collections of such dialogues were published in magazines, and for a time the *Boston Herald* printed two or three dialogues a week on the editorial page.[52]

Bradford greatly enjoyed writing his dialogues, thought well of them on the whole, and would have been glad to have a booklength collection published. The opinions of others were divided; some admired the dialogues greatly, while others thought them trifling, pointless, or undeveloped, and Bradford sardonically recognized the latter point of view by using as an epigraph for the chapbook Davenant's "This laconic ass makes brevity ridiculous."

The dialogues were not modeled upon Landor's *Imaginary Conversations*, which Bradford thought "among the splendid things in English prose, but as dialogues . . . mostly, to my mind, forlorn failures, having no semblance of human reality or truth, . . . point, sparkle, or naturalness of their speech."[53] The sketches vary considerably in quality. Some were intended merely to amuse the author and his friends, while others have considerable bite. The most general shortcoming is lack of climax. Among the most brilliant are those between Byron and Augusta Leigh, Byron and his biographer Ethel Colburn Mayne, Lamb and Macaulay, and

Moody and Keats; the one between John Fletcher and Bradford himself is good criticism.[54] Naturally those in which he himself figures are especially interesting to students of his work and personality. In one Mrs. Ripley and Aunt Clara Kinsman speculate about his future "while G.B., aged two, plays about the floor." George Agassiz and Sam Eliot give a most unflattering picture of him in his youth. He resurrects the mother he never knew for a dialogue in which she tells him she is proud of him, and there are dialogues in which two whom he had loved in youth talk about him as they walk away from his funeral, in which he paddles Lincoln and Shakespeare in a canoe on the Avon, and in which he tells Jules Lemaître that he has meant more to him than even Sainte-Beuve. "I am not like him, as I am like you."[55]

So much, then, for the psychographs. What, now, in closing, of the psychographer?

Chapter Eight

The Man

Tastes and Temperament

When a high-school girl in Arkansas wrote Bradford in connection with an assignment, he replied:

> I am fearfully old. I have blue eyes. I am an invalid most of the time and ill tempered all the time. I like cats and dislike children. My house is full of books, but they are all old books, and I read the same over and over, and know nothing of all the nonsense that goes on in the world. I belong to the Victorian age, which you have heard your grandmother tell about, when people wore long hair and long skirts and retired instead of going to bed and mostly pretended to be better than they really were. Now they pretend to be worse, but I don't see that it makes very much difference, because it is all pretty much pretending anyway.[1]

He lived for beauty, love, and glory, and he was quite right when he said that he had the intensity of genius even if he lacked the talent. His tremendous zest shows in his capacity for absorption in every new project, the necessity which rested upon him to get at it and get it done as soon as it was suggested to him, even in the incapacity to muster the patience which produces perfection that he attributed to himself; and if all this forms an unbelievable contrast to the depression he was also capable of suffering, perhaps we should remember that depression, too, is a form of intensity. When he was twenty, he began writing an autobiography, but decided to give it up until he was older and calmer. Many years later, rereading the passage which records this resolution, he added a note: "Oh, God, when will it ever be? More morbid, more egotistical, more introspective, and far less calm, after forty years, than I was then."[2] By this time his life was outwardly restricted, regulated to the minutest degree by the clock, and many would have called it dull. "Yet, by God! no, there is nothing dull about it; it is a whirlpool of torment and anxieties and questions and vain efforts and unreasonable childish despairs, and flashed through and through at moments with strange, unearthly gleams of alluring beauty and hope and excitement, that I will not deny."[3]

He could worry himself sick about anything or nothing. One of his manuscripts is sold for seventy-five dollars, and he worries about whether he should include an estimate of the value of his manuscripts in his personal property-tax returns. Somebody casts doubt upon the financial security of the Book League, of which he is an editor, and he worries about his liability in case of a crash, whether he ought to have their house put in his wife's name, and whether, if it came to the worst, everything would go or only his share.

He blames himself for the lack of self-control manifested in such tendencies, yet when he could not sleep at night, he was capable of lying perfectly still, turning once each half-hour by the striking of the clock, and focusing his thoughts. The last year of his life he was still struggling in to Boston by train, though his wife was willing to drive him, because he thought that so long as he could make it on his own, he should. "Never under any circumstances give in to these moods, never have. If I had, I should have accomplished nothing."[4] So he dictated portions of *A Prophet of Joy* from his bed when he was too sick to lift his head from the pillow.

The curse of his life was the severe aural vertigo which seized him from time to time, sometimes prostrating him for weeks. In June 1931, he recorded that he had had his first attack just twenty-seven years before, but in July 1922, he had dated his first attack 1889. The trouble was in his right ear, and he could tell when it threatened to come on by the condition of his hearing. "If the clock is dead, so am I, incapable of serious interest in my own life or in that of others, bent only on listening and fearing." When he lay awake at night, he listened "for the steady ticktock of my little French timepiece, and when I can hear it, it is the greatest of luxuries, and when it is lost, my hope and almost my soul are lost with it."[5] Different diagnoses were made by aurist, orthopedist, dietician, and others, including one young man who was sure the whole trouble was psychosomatic, and there were a number of minor operations which might bring temporary relief but no permanent cure. Thus from the spring of 1914 to that of 1917 he had no trouble. Summer brought constant threats but no attacks. During the winter of 1917–18 he was well again, but in the spring he had several violent attacks, and through the following winter he was confined to the house and pretty much to his bed. In May he made his first trip to Boston since the preceding August. And so it went through the years.

I fix myself in the morning before my big desk, right next to the bed, with a great rocking chair on the other side of me, with a thick quilt in it, so that if I fall over, I shall not quite bang hard against the floor. Then I pound *Pepys* off on the typewriter as best I can, when every instant it seems as if my head would fall off, and I cannot turn it to either side without peril of losing it altogether.[6]

Among the other diseases and malfunctions doctors found in him were ptosis of the intestines, an enlarged colon, a dislocated stomach, an excess of thyroid secretions, rheumatism, neuritis, sciatica, and anemia. Besides all this, there was a high susceptibility to grippe. Despite its raw east winds, Bradford loved March ("the charm of it . . . is in the light, in the broad sweep of the ascending sun, unobstructed by any of the leafage which brings a different sort of charm in June"),[7] but the winter often brought a heavy grippe which might leave sequelae behind it, besides a general feeling of depletion and discouragement. In January 1926, grippe and an abscessed ear broke in on *Darwin*, just as he was beginning to write, and he lost nine pounds in a week. When he tried to come downstairs to dinner the last Christmas day of his life, he broke down with an hysterical fit of weeping, yet by the beginning of January he was studying Portuguese and looking forward to the proofs of *Saints and Sinners* and to getting his ledgers ready for income-tax purposes, and was besides "crazy to get to work" on "Creation," the book he did not live to write.

When courage ebbed, he would complain about all this. "The whole history of my life has been something that I wanted to do and couldn't, because I was not well enough."[8] Again, he would tell himself that he had been very fortunate, that nearly all his troubles had been his own fault, and even that perhaps it might have been a good thing for him to have some real difficulty to keep his mind off little things! Even his special malady could be treated at times with bravado: "What do I care for vertigo, a pleasant little revolution in a world otherwise abominably stagnant."[9]

So, though he might sometimes cry out for death—

> Sleep is better than loveless days,
> Death is better than sleep[10]

—he never meant it for long, and suicide never tempted him. He shrank from change, and, like Hamlet, he knew not what might come after death; if life was terrible, death might be even worse; lovely as Mount Auburn was, it must be horribly cold in winter. "You mustn't take my pessimism too seriously, as I do not myself."[11] In *Portraits of Women*, he spoke of "those great passions and little pleasures which to some of us seem to fill every cranny of life with business and delight" and of art as "to some a resource so great that it overcomes not only tedium but even misery and acute suffering."[12] In 1929 he hoped not to see another winter, "though at the same time I should like to write Saints and Sinners and the volume of artists and the volume of Loves and Hates, so life and death are queerly complicated after all."[13]

Besides art, what refuge did he have? He thought himself an ignorant, incompetent observer of nature compared to Thoreau or Roosevelt, yet his response to natural beauty was rapturous. "Yesterday I spent the day on the river with G[am] and what a day!

Such sky, such sunlight! Such a gorgeous glow of the foliage, so rich and fresh from all the rain!"[14] This was early; but as long as he lived, he could extract the same rapture from watching the trees and the sky and the clouds from his hammock on the porch. Mountains he liked best at a distance; their nearness overwhelmed him; but he always loved the sea. Nor did he stop with exclaiming over beauties. Many of his editorials in the *Boston Herald* deal with nature, and close observation is indicated in them. When a friend was in Europe in 1925, he wrote him astonishingly detailed memories of his own stay there, so many years before, covering nature as well as architecture, objets d'art, and much besides.

Yet nature frightened him, too. As a small child, he would not go out to play because he was afraid of the birds, and even in later years he carefully avoided dogs on his walks. When, in his youth, he sometimes inadvertently touched young birds in a nest, it gave him the horrors. "And to touch any minute, fragile creature gives me the same sort of shudder today. I cannot bear to do it. I think that is something the explanation, though it never occurred to me before; that there is a certain sacred terror about life, which makes me shrink from too close contact with it."[15] On the whole, he got on best with cats, which Mrs. Bradford adored. As he wrote in 1930 to Jessie P. Buford:

I was much interested in your cat letter and should have been glad to read it to my own feline friend, but he is somewhat of a misanthropic disposition and might not have taken it kindly. He does sit regularly at table and has learned to kiss his mistress before she gives him a tid-bit, but he does not get all his meals in that way as it is rather more convenient to serve him at a side table. I cannot say that I have ever had any great taste for pets. At least, I am so constitutionally indolent that I shrink from the trouble they involve. But I have always liked to have a cat about, perhaps the least troublesome of all, and as a boy I was very fond of my dogs and horses, though I have never been able to relish the dogs of other people.[16]

In his youth, Bradford seems to have participated, or tried to participate, in almost all the sports that were open to country boys in his time—swimming, sailing, coasting, skating. He played tennis, croquet, and baseball, and later golf, all eagerly, he says, but very badly, and, in the late 1890s, together with much of the rest of the population, he became a bicycle enthusiast. Once, at least, in the 1880s, he visited a roller skating rink, where they skated to music, which affected him like art and made him think of Shelley and Chopin. Perhaps swimming was what he did best. He learned at five, and having learned, was in fresh water nearly every day, avoiding salt water as too cold and sticky. In later years, swimming was denied him because of his ear and nearly everything else involving physical exertion by limitations of strength, though only a few months before his death, he says he would like to have a billiard table if there were room for it and he were not too weak. We hear of dancing parties, too, and when he visited New York in 1925, he sat in the great dining room of the hotel to watch the dancing. Though he carefully avoided learning bridge, he did play whist and cribbage, and in the 1920s he speaks with amazing tolerance of the crossword-puzzle idiocy.

But the abiding passion was baseball. For ten or fifteen years, he went ten or a dozen times each summer to Fenway Park, relishing both the dexterity of the players and the rudeness and vulgarity of the crowds. He watched both boys and girls practice baseball and basketball at the local high school, and once he became so agitated over what he considered an unfair play by a visiting team that a policeman laid his hand on his shoulder! "I don't believe anybody ever had the passion for contests in a higher degree than I have," he writes,[17] and if this seems hard to reconcile with his dominant interests, it is probably quite in tune with the intensity which inspired his inordinate thirst for glory and turned him into the self tormentor he became.

Relations with Others

The sympathetic humanity of Bradford's study of human beings in his psychographs has been sufficiently brought out in the preceding chapters. He valued such sympathy in those he read and deplored its absence when he failed to find it, approving of the "new biography" only "when it tends not to drag the great down, but to lift us up. To show that saints and heroes are human, is not to show that saintliness and heroism are cheap, common, empty, worthless. It is rather to show that the possibilities of these great things are inherent in our humanity as well as theirs."[18] Even M. R. Werner, contemplating a book on Tammany Hall, must be admonished not to permit "the undeniable degradation of human nature" to drive him into "too great bitterness. . . . You have not patience enough with the deplorable, delightful failings of humanity."[19]

Bradford himself was troubled because he thought the kindliness of his writings did not sufficiently carry over into his private life. When somebody he disliked suffered misfortune, though he was sure he would have done anything in his power to prevent it, he still felt there was something in him that was pleased, and sometimes he even derived a pleasing excitement from public calamity. Moreover, instead of dismissing such thoughts from his mind, as other people do, he dwelt upon them and analyzed them and reflected upon how contemptible they made him out. Mrs. Bradford never wearied in practical benevolences, from which he was cut off by his health, his lack of practical efficiency, and his difficulty in social relationships, and he never ceased to dwell, to his own disparagement, on the differences between them in this regard.

Yet he was often deeply moved by sufferings and tragedies quite alien to himself, as when a boy and girl in the neighborhood, eighteen and fifteen, committed suicide together. And there were problems with which he could help or try to. He once invited a Harvard law student who was worrying about whether he should marry an Irish Catholic girl to come to him to talk the matter over, and when a youngster he knew was trying to start a literary magazine, he went the length of soliciting advertising from Harpers and Houghton Mifflin. He agreed to judge a short-story contest, though he felt himself incompetent, because he loved the high school, and he probably never left even an impertinent letter unanswered. He sent books to people who brazenly begged for them, and he even replied courteously to one illiterate scribbler who thought he was a crank who ought to have fought for the Confederacy—in his perambulator, presumably.

But of course his principal benevolence was exercised in his indefatigable attempts to help young writers. He had no confidence in his ability to help people get published, but he never ceased trying. A lady in Missouri wanted him to teach her to write poetry for a fee. He told her it could not be taught and refused the fee but encouraged her to send him manuscripts, only to find that all her poems were about lilies and lilacs. He sent her *Shadow Verses* and urged her to write about her own experiences; then he learned that she was a tubercular paralytic and felt that he had been brutal. And when a former neighbor sent him a collection of poems she had managed to have published, he wrote an unsolicited review of it for the *New York Evening Post* and sent her a copy. "I know such a thing would have delighted me twenty years ago, and more and more I feel anxious to do any little thing I can to ease the hell of doubt and struggle that I myself went through for so many years."[20]

Yet social contacts were very hard for him. He did better with one person than with a group, but he often complains that he can get no intimate or meaningful talk even with those he values most. He was distressed by his feeling that all he knew how to do was ask questions, and he feared this might estrange people, yet he shrank from bringing up his own concerns unless they were asked for.

He was uneasy with Ellery Sedgwick, because he never felt he could depend upon him, and with Ferris Greenslet, who frightened him, but even friends like Bliss Perry, M. A. DeWolfe Howe, and Katharine Lee Bates put him on his guard. In a way he felt himself part of the New England aristocracy, and intellectually he knew he was superior to most of it, yet in the presence of men like Robert Grant and Barrett Wendell he felt that he lacked savoir faire, even to his manners, voice, and clothes.

The first time Robert Frost came to the house, he found him somewhat lacking in humor and grooming and a little affected, though not nearly so much so as Vachel Lindsay or W. B. Yeats.

Later he came to like him but reproached himself for deferring to him. With Edwin Arlington Robinson he got on even better, in spite of, or perhaps because of, the fact that Robinson was quite as shy as he was, and with Carl Sandburg, who was a little uncouth, but quite without Lindsay's stridency, he achieved considerable interchange. Actually Bradford felt no real humility in his own mind even in the presence of men of the world whose competence was different in kind from that of any writer. Thus James Michael Curley, the Massachusetts politico, was judged to have humor and sympathy without great intelligence or refinement, and Colonel House was credited with vast knowledge of the world but little book learning.

In sharp contrast to Bradford's discomfort in general social relations, he could pour himself out in letters, even to strangers. "I write letters to my imagination," he admits.[21] But his gift for self-reproach being what it was, he got little comfort out of this, for he calls himself hypocritical, cold-hearted, and self-absorbed, with no real affection for his correspondents, and a spiritual chameleon. He also admitted frankly that he enjoyed being lionized and felt more at home with those who flattered and caressed him than with equals or superiors. Though he was embarrassed by one southern lady who kissed him ("it is no use, I am not a social being, kissed or not"),[22] he could stand purring and cooing even from elderly ladies who professed to admire him, though he admits he preferred the young and pretty ones.

Bradford was no hermit, by either nature or practice. One Christmas there were nine houseguests, of whom four were children, and once there were sixty to Thanksgiving dinner. He had intended to go to bed early, but he stayed up, even playing the Virginia reel for them, and enjoyed it all. Obviously, hard as human contacts were for him, he craved them, for he was forever inviting people to come to see him, often for extended stays; yet when they came he could not wait to get them out of the house again, partly because he was a slave to the routine with which they interfered and partly because of the strain of being with them. Once he even writes of his oldest and closest friend that he never sees him come without wondering when he will leave.

The sad thing about all this is that it was so unnecessary. Even when he had house guests, he continued to work as much as his strength permitted, and there is abundant testimony that his visitors never sensed the tension under which he labored. In 1930, when he was comparatively well, he made a deliberate effort, with his wife's encouragement, to get out and about more, and enjoyed it sufficiently so that he wondered whether he was not turning into a social butterfly and made his reader wonder whether, if he had done this kind of thing more often, he might not have been better off. He once had a long and interesting talk in the train with a mechanic from Natick who had been an exhibition dancer, and when a twenty-year-old movie fan who had sold a large number of stories to the magazines came to see him one night, they talked for two hours, and he found he had seldom enjoyed anything more. It is clear that the basic difficulty, as he always recognized when writing about other persons similarly constituted, was his own intense self-consciousness, the feeling that he was not making a good impression or doing himself justice. Indeed, he recognized it in himself also, "the detestable intrusion of my wretched, insignificant, too significant self, which bores me and bothers me and distracts me."[23] But here, unfortunately, as with all other personal shortcomings and idiosyncrasies, recognition was easier than cure, for him as for others.

The Citizen

As for men in their larger social relations, Bradford had political views and took a reasonable interest in public affairs, but politics can hardly be called one of his great interests. Nor did his performance in this area add much to his stature. For thirty years he voted Democratic, "taking my stand upon what I regarded to be the essential Democratic principles, the limitation of government interference and especially the assertion of State Rights."[24] After

that, the Democrats seemed to him to have abandoned their tradi-
tional stand, and the Republicans impressing him as, on the whole,
the more effective administrators, he changed his affiliation. He
was a strong believer in the two-party system and inclined to criticize those who refused to ally themselves with either party and vote
for "the best man," though he admitted that "the safety-valve of
the party system lies in the ... small shifting minority that refuses
to be dictated to and is always ready to switch over when either
party grows too wilful and tyrannous."[25] As has already been
pointed out, he inherited his father's ideas about bringing the
executive branch into the legislature, and he came to life notably on
this issue in 1924, when Senator James Couzens showed an interest
in it; indeed he had already tried to persuade Sedgwick to get either
William Howard Taft or Nicholas Murray Butler, both of whom
favored it, to do an *Atlantic* article. He saw the Constitution as
based upon a reasonable balance of state and federal powers and was
much concerned about the steady encroachment of the federal. In
his more pessimistic moments, he saw this as having perhaps already gone so far that the state governments had become moribund
and might just as well be abolished, though he shrank from the con-
fusion and possible consequences of a new Constitutional convention.

On some issues on which he did not feel strongly, such as the
Wilson League of Nations versus Harding's World Court, Bradford could coyly plead ignorance as an excuse for not taking a stand,
but this disqualification did not trouble him when he was really interested. He was lukewarm on woman suffrage, thinking it would
effect no important changes and seeing no advantage in merely
swelling the voting rolls, but he was strongly opposed to the soldiers' bonus and the child-labor amendment, and he claimed to have
foretold the 1929 crash five years in advance.

Bradford hated war; after World War I was over, he could not
even bear to read about it. Yet he too often takes his stand with the
"I hate war but" people. The very year he died, he refused to sign
an appeal to the disarmament conference at Geneva, on the ground
that peaceable peoples could not avoid protecting themselves so long

as there were "robber nations as well as individuals, Japans and Mussolinis and Soviets," and he added, devastatingly, that the mitigation of war's evils was "a matter for careful and scientific study by trained experts, not for ministers and hysterical women."[26] In *As God Made Them*, he shrugs off Henry Clay's responsibility for the War of 1812 on the ground that though not of great importance in itself, it did contribute to the prestige of this country, and in the Civil War books he enters with surprising sympathy into the battle lust of several generals.

As for World War I, though in 1903 he had sympathetically reviewed Wolf von Shierbrand's collection of the Kaiser's speeches, gagging at the monarch's royal pride, but seeing him as a virtuous man, sincerely devoted to peace, he inherited hatred of Prussia and the Hohenzollerns from his father, and as late as 1923, he was clinging to the now completely discredited view that Germany, and the Kaiser specifically, were solely responsible for the war and wishing that both Kaiser and Crown Prince had shared the fate of the Czar. In his psychograph of Wilson he begs the whole question of American involvement by writing that Wilson was "finally compelled to join the Allies,"[27] and his long review of Howe's five-volume *Memoirs of the Harvard Dead* has abundant praise of heroism and far too little realization of its futility and shameful waste. Of what the soldiers themselves wrote, he says that "in the main there is only a passionately loyal devotion to country and cause, a sense that the one important thing is to do the duty of the hour, no matter what it is or whither it leads, and to leave the rest to those whom it concerns, or to God."[28] It would be difficult to find a more effective formula for destruction.

When Bradford was young, he entertained certain tendencies toward radicalism. His later conservatism he tried to justify on the ground that his nihilism was so overwhelming that what ordinary reformers proposed failed to move him. He never ceased to regard himself as a parasite and cumberer of the earth, and he admitted freely that he refused to consider new ideas because they might demand sacrifices he was not prepared to make. He shied from the conservatism of Calvin Coolidge, and those who wished to edit

school textbooks in the interest of political orthodoxy got no support from him. He was glad to be in the American Academy because
it was not pleasant to be left out, but he was not overimpressed by
that august body, nor was it the only such upon which he looked
with unanointed eyes. Thus the Massachusetts Historical Society
was "something which looks grand and impressive from the outside
and which one is eager to enter, but which, once in, one finds a
good deal of a bore," and he was sure that sufficient contact with
the trustees of his beloved Athenaeum would make a Robespierre of
him.[29] "Let us look upon these eager, furious young radicals with
all the sympathy we can," he wrote Howe, "and only wish we were
young and furious. . . . It is the radical who makes the world go,
after all, while we miserable conservatives . . . just sit on the brake
and hold it back." And he could even write in an editorial:

We say that in this country all men have equal opportunity. Do they? Is
it equal opportunity for thrift and intelligence to be born under a
crowding, hopeless burden of exacting, excessive toil, while vice and
incapacity inherit millions? We say that in this country all men are
equal before the law. Are they? Is it equality before the law when rich
men can clog, pervert, and corrupt the processes of justice, while poor
men are condemned and punished often beyond their deserts?[30]

Nevertheless the conservatism was there. Bradford consistently
took a dim view of Thomas Jefferson. His article on La Follette admits the need of reform but stresses the dangers of destruction more.
At the beginning of the 1920s, he was much upset over what he
considered the pro-German and pro-Soviet tendencies of the *Nation*,
and a few years later he called John Haynes Holmes a ghastly
radical. When Mark Van Doren asked him to recommend books for
translation into Russian, he complied, adding, somewhat irrelevantly,
that he was not "a great admirer of the Soviet Republic, which my
rather stupid old conservatism is inclined to regard as a gang of
robbers and cutthroats."[31]

He admitted that large fortunes might need to be curbed and
controlled, but insisted that "a very large part, perhaps the larger

part of the capital of the country is in the hands of small holders," and he looked to these "for the safe, moderate, conservative handling of political issues."[32] When the Sacco-Vanzetti case came along, he admitted that he could form no judgment as to the guilt or innocence of the accused but found himself exasperated "by the impertinent interference of the whole world with what is strictly a Massachusetts matter," and, even though he disliked "condemnations upon merely circumstancial evidence," he could still "see nothing to be done but execute the creatures, and it is certainly not in any way possible for the authorities to give in now." Yet the next year, when he read the Sacco-Vanzetti letters, he found it hard to believe they had been written by criminals.[33]

There are also unfortunate traces of race and class and section, not in Bradford's published writings but in his letters and journals. He could congratulate Louis Untermeyer upon "the boldness and freedom of your racial stand" and tell him that the future lay "not perhaps with the Jews especially, but with the coming American race of which you must be a large ingredient and which must be established by the most vigorous and intense of the racial characteristics of each people."[34] And having called Sarah Bernhardt "a cheap Greenwich Village Bohemian Jew," he could wonder whether he was not himself "an irretrievable snob" and explain that he did not mind her humble origin, which was no more so than his own, nor her eccentricity, which he enjoyed, but merely "a certain strain of vulgarity which is just as likely to be found in Hyde Park or Beacon Street as in Greenwich Village and in a high-church Episcopalian as a Jew."[35] But while he could get such things straight intellectually, he never got them straight emotionally. As he felt, not reasoned, there were no people like his people and no place like New England, and it pleased him when the sailors he and his wife entertained in wartime nearly all had "thoroughly American" names— "only two, or possible three, out of the nine, Irish, and one German. They came all from the eastern part of the country, but none from west of the Mississippi except one from Texas."[36] He even attributes a certain roughness to the Middle West, though

granting some delicacy to Californians, and he wrote of one girl
interviewer that "she was New York, but not offensively."[37]

The Private Man

But Bradford, like other men, had a body as well as a mind,
emotions as well as ideas. In 1927 he recorded that when he was
young, eating was his main interest, and it is true that in the early
days he sometimes complains of indigestion and sick headache,
brought on, he thought, by overeating. In later years, he was able
to eat very little—a hearty breakfast, he says, and after that only
enough to sustain life. He loved sweet potatoes, baked beans, and
cheese, and looked forward to eating them in heaven, since they
did not agree with him here. There are few references to tobacco,
and alcohol was never a problem to him, though he seems to have
had no strict antiliquor principles, since, in 1884, when he eschewed
alcohol under Helen's influence, he said that he himself had a
stronger feeling against meat, and in 1921 he was avoiding both
meat and fish on account of disgust. In Prohibition times, the conviction that liquor was a scourge among men kept him from con-
demning the Volstead Act, much as he disliked reformers. "If prohibition affected candy," he writes, "it would be a much worse blow
to me than any denial of alcohol; for I have never been able to get
any taste for anything but the very sweetest and lightest of wines,
and I prefer a soda any day to these. But candy has always been
my dream."[38]

Sex was much more important. Looking back in age upon his
early life, he declared that, proper as his conduct had been, he was
always subject to its dominion. Clearly he thought our bodies more
chaste than our souls, and he early distinguished between love and
passion. "I have never loved but one woman in my life. As for passion, it is properly the manifestation of love, but when one cannot
spend it on whom one loves, the weak heart sometimes lets it go to
others. It flashes up for an instant and is gone."[39]

He once proposed calling a volume of lyrics "God, Girls, and
Gamaliel," but Mrs. Bradford put a stop to that.[40] There are many

lyrics which would have felt at home in such a collection, and there are even indications·that the writing of such poems may have served as a safety-valve:

> I look always, don't you see,
>   For a cure for thinking,
> I suppose the best would be
>   Alcoholic drinking.
>
> I've not come to drinking yet,
>   Songs of sinful kisses
> Somehow help me to forget
>   Thought and its abysses.[41]

Quite as interesting as the poems, however, is his discussion of a musical comedy he saw in 1926:

I find a strange, vast excitement, in the whirl of naked limbs, the delicious mingling of the colors, and through it all the glimmering ecstasy of the wild dance music. The faces and the words are horrible, yet they enthrall me, simply because they are average humanity, . . . and that I love, more indeed at a distance than in too near contact, but still love, waywardly, profoundly, from the consciousness that I always have of its near relation to myself. I feel always that it would be such a slight transition for me to step into this whirl, to cast off my strict, secluded propriety, and fling myself into the mad oblivion of all this folly and vice and dissipation.[42]

But the reservations here are more significant than the longing. Even under the spell of the attraction, he knows that he likes all this best "at a distance." Surely these faces cannot all have been "horrible," nor can all these actors have been given up to "vice and dissipation." Even in his journal, he cannot bring himself to call the girls' bare legs "legs," and instead uses "limbs," like a Victorian lady novelist. All in all, one can hardly feel that he was in great danger of flinging himself "into the mad oblivion." Indeed we know from other evidence that his own body was strange to him, "pitiable, I would say disgusting, but the strangeness is more than the disgust,"[43] and that he never felt alive until he had got his clothes on. He thought he ought to look into Havelock Ellis before writing the second chapter of *Life and I* but could not bring himself to do so, no doubt because of "too great and morbid sensual propensities of my own."[44] He found polygamy so disgusting that he almost refused to review Werner's biography of Brigham Young, and he nearly resigned his Book League editorship because he disapproved of many of the new books they published. Indeed he was even offended by the "sexual implication" in *Dear Old Templeton* by his friend Alice Brown, whose very title nauseated him, it is hard to see why.[45] On the other hand, he did go to bat for one Book League selection, *Grim Youth*, which George Herbert Palmer condemned, and his review of V. F. Calverton's *Three Strange Loves* shows a sympathetic understanding of the wildest vagaries. It is true that he could make terms with indecency somewhat more comfortably in the literature of the past, but he was in character when he found Casanova desperately dull even when most lascivious and rejoiced that the manuscript of his memoirs was safe in the Brockhaus safe, where he hoped it would remain undisturbed until somebody had sense enough to burn it.

Bradford's attitude toward women in general was mixed. In one editorial he credits them with surpassing men in "enthusiasm, self-sacrifice, idealism, and a hatred of unworthy compromise,"[46] and nobody could show a greater appreciation of the problems of mothers and housewives or manifest a more generous recognition of the fact that a woman must bring more to marriage than a man and that when it succeeds the greater credit must go to her. Yet there are many passages at which feminists must gag. He was irritated by old women who dressed like young ones and by women who laughed and shrieked in conversation even when nothing amusing had been said, and he seems to have felt that women devoured the modern sex novels with prurient curiosity. In one of his dialogues he makes Shakespeare say that he drew women out of his imagination because he knew only men in life. They "were all far off, and lovely, and I made them so. If only they were true!"[47] Worse still is his

commentary on a novel the Book League was considering, which
he called "hopelessly feminine."

It has woman, woman stamped all over it, and while I am by no means a
misogynist, I do think woman a vilely disturbing influence in our civilization at present. I am inclined to think we should do well to get her
out of politics and art into the domestic sphere where she came from.[48]

Both Bradford's poems and his journal show something of an
obsession with "the low-necked, short-skirted, bare-legged" girls of
today; there is even one extreme reference to the "noisy and drunken
flappers in the street [who] do not seem to care much for God except to take his name in vain."[49] The same tendency shows in his
comparisons between such women as George Sand and Ninon de
Lenclos and "New York" or "college" girls in *Daughters of Eve*.
The legs seem to have been particularly difficult for him, though no
doubt the frequency with which he notices them shows interest. In
1931 he wrote, "If God and long skirts and female virtue should
come back, wouldn't it be queer—and disconcerting?"[50] One wonders where, in his secluded life, he can possibly have encountered
these shocking creatures, since whenever he did meet girls, whether
they came from Wellesley College or interviewed him for New York
papers, he was impressed by their quietness, refinement, and good
manners; yet no matter how often this happened, he seems always
to have been surprised by it. Certainly he got on better with girls
than with boys, whom he seems to have relished only on the athletic
field, and there are many passages in both prose and verse which
say that, underneath all the changes in their clothes and manners,
girls are still very much what they always were.

Of Bradford's very successful marriage to Helen Hubbard Ford,
perhaps enough has been said in Chapter 1. In his "Early Journal"
he credited himself with a real "elective affinity" for her (he had
been reading Goethe). "And of all the numerous women I have
been in love with (with many far more passionately than with
Helen) I do not think that there was one with whom I found this

subtle union." He expected the passion between them to die out in time, leaving "sympathy and union and communion of our whole souls," but if he had married Lottie Plumer or Sallie Ames, only "satiety and disgust" would have succeeded. He feared that he might have been a little unfaithful to Helen with Lottie, not in his heart but in his senses. If he were to die, he said, three words would be found on his heart: Poetry, Helen, and Wellesley Hills. He thought he was echoing Mary Queen of Scots; actually it was only Mary Tudor.[51]

It may seem odd that when he mentioned Lottie and Sallie, he did not also mention Helen's older sister Harriet, later Harriet Ford Cutler, for in 1929 he wrote that he had been in love with her for four years beginning just fifty years ago, and in a dialogue written the next year he made it five years, adding that he did not know whether he had liked her for her honesty, brains, or sexual or spiritual fascination. When he was in Europe in 1878–79, he wrote to Harriet, not Helen, but after the former had come over to join him and his father, their relations were never very close again until after he had married her sister, and in 1896 their correspondence, which was in large part his solo performance, was renewed. Though he never ceased to think of her affectionately, in later years, after she had died, he was sure that her memory was better than her actual presence would have been, and even while she was alive, he had enjoyed writing to her more than talking with her.

But Helen's charm for him never faded. Perhaps the best calm, considered expression of his mature devotion to her comes in what he wrote H. L. Mencken upon the latter's marriage:

Bernard Shaw tells us that no man can give his real opinion of marriage so long as his wife is alive and marriage, like all other earthly things, has its undeniable drawbacks. But I have been married forty-five years, and my adoration of my wife, my enormous dependence upon her, both spiritual and material, are even more than they were forty-five years ago. The great horror of my life is that one of us must go first, and I —selfishly—pray God . . . that it may be I.[52]

Because of his invalidism, his physical dependence was greater than that of most husbands, but his spiritual dependence was hardly less complete, and since he left no facet of his character and experience unplumbed, he was always painfully conscious of the selfish element in his devotion. Though he was thinking of religion when he wrote the following words, it is clear that he thought the same considerations applied to human love also:

My beloved Fénelon insists upon the propriety and necessity of loving God for himself. Alas, I fear I am quite incapable of anything of the kind. Such love as is within my power, and this has always been deplorably little, is utterly and wholly selfish and incurably tangled up with what I can get out of it.[53]

He claimed to "detest babies" and to have "no faculty with children, no tact, and very little pleasure,"[54] and one feels that he must have left his own very much to his wife. His daughter, who became a teacher, never gave him any anxiety except because of her delicate health, but his son's suicide was the greatest shock he ever experienced. Nineteen years after the event, he analyzed his feelings about this as he analyzed everything else:

I suppose I should say . . . that that event blighted my life completely. But I cannot say anything of the kind. Gam was a sweet, noble, pure, sensitive nature, and I never had anything whatever to complain of in his conduct toward me, though I cannot say as much of my conduct toward him. But he and I were totally different. He was far more like my father. . . . I am more and more convinced of my utter incapability of the simple natural human affections and of my immense, engrossing, total absorption in myself. In a sense it may be that my affection for H[elen] is so huge and so involving that it leaves room for nothing else. But, as I often point out to her, that affection is so damnably complicated with infinitely varied need that it is vexatiously impossible to tell where need ends and affection begins. . . . I did not need Gam, and I need no human being except H[elen], and after the first overwhelming shock Gam's death brought me little except a certain financial relief in no way comparable to that which I . . . experienced shortly after when my father died. . . . I do not think I ever got much pleasure from my children, though I feel that on the whole I was a fairly de-

voted father. For S[ally]'s sake, I should be glad to have her have
children, if she wants them, but to me the thought of grandchildren
is a mere nuisance and horror. I do not want the burden and worry of
them and I do not in the least understand the eagerness with which my
father looked forward to his, nor, I am sure, should I find the least bit
of the pleasure which they gave him. The truth is, my whole life is in
my literary ambition. I have no other life, and never shall have.[55]

He and Helen went to Mount Auburn every year on the anni-
versary of Gam's death. The inscription on his tombstone is from
Beaumont:

> 'Tis not a life,
> 'Tis but a piece of childhood thrown away.

The Fight for Glory

"Ah, it is indeed life, this writing business. . . . During that hour
of writing, though it tires my back till it almost seems as if it would
split in pieces, I really live. During the remainder of the day, I
merely exist."[56] Unless he was prostrated, not even illness was allowed to interfere. "In fact, I think the rule is to work twice as hard
when one is ill, so as to forget all about it."[57]

He preferred poetry, fiction, and drama to psychography because
it meant continuous writing, while with psychography there were
long intervals of preparation, but he admitted that psychography
was, for this reason, better suited to his limitations of strength.
Practically all his writing was done in the morning, and since everything was planned out minutely in his head before he came to his
typewriter it proceeded rapidly. He was sure he did his best work
"when I am swept away by the rapture of momentary impulse and
pour out the flaming words as fast as I can set them down," admitting that lack of revision might be his weak point, "yet I find
so little to revise."[58]

He insists that he wrote for glory. "My object is first, last, and
always to glorify myself and I should not be in the least tempted

to do the work if it did not lead to that end."[59] Yet when a Duke student wrote to say that his books had made him a better man, he was deeply moved.

Sometimes he is sure he is a complete failure who will be altogether forgotten in fifty years; again he looks forward to his publishers selling thousands of sets of his complete works. If there is a consistent pattern, he generally thought well of his work upon completing it, found it dull as ditchwater in proof, and enjoyed it upon later rereading.

Take his comments upon individual works out of context, unmodified by the self-disparagement expressed elsewhere, and you will set him down a colossal egotist if not a megalomaniac. *American Portraits, 1875–1900* is "a superb book." He does not know where to look for "more brilliant, more subtle, more glorified work." (For all that, he thought it would probably be the last book Houghton Mifflin would accept.) *Darwin* is "a monumental book," and if one wants a book about Pepys at all, it is hard to see how anyone could write "a more brilliant and effective one" than his. So too with the unappreciated creative works. *A Prophet of Joy* "will certainly go down to posterity, even if it does not sell now." The dialogue of *Matthew Porter* is extraordinary and the characters not far behind it. And he quotes two verses from "A Duchess of Dreams" and exclaims, "Ah, what exquisite lines, are they not?"[60]

He admired his letters and incidental writings as much as his formal works and had them bound and preserved, though without correcting typing errors, and he gave much thought to who should edit his literary remains, the same persons being chosen and rejected in different pages of his journal. His admiration for his incidental writings he sometimes manages, characteristically, to turn to self-disparagement—"I am inclined to think editorials and reviews are the things I do best: they suit my slapdash, haphazard style"[61]— and he half boasts and half confesses that when the *Atlantic* sends him a book on Rasputin, he reads it "in three scraps of evenings, knowing nothing about the subject before and precious little more after, but I write a most brilliant extempore review, on the basis of a plan conceived, as usual, before I opened the book at all."[62]

He wept over the charmingly pathetic ending of *Early Days in Wellesley* and thought a Memorial Day editorial for the *Youth's Companion* superior to the Gettysburg Address and hard to beat in English prose.

Disparagement might be sparked by reading some contemporary like Strachey or Robert Graves who, he thought, was doing something he could not match. Then he had "nothing but a petty talent, and a man has to have more than a petty talent to crowd his way to the front today." And he would conclude reluctantly that he was a kind of Henry Cabot Lodge in literature—"a perfectly mediocre and average man, with every possible advantage of education, position, and circumstances, who by these advantages shoulders himself with assiduous labor into a fair but after all utterly mediocre position."[63] And though he did not always think thus of his talent, he was fairly consistent in his evaluation of his character. Those who admired him, he thought, must all be unbalanced. "I do not admire myself. At least, if I do, it is not for the things they profess to admire. They admire my character. My character! God save the mark! As if I ever had any to begin with, and if I have any whatever, it is certainly not admirable."[64]

In the "Haunted Biographer" dialogues, he makes Sarah Ripley speak of "that keen-sighted nephew," and Sainte-Beuve tells her that he has inherited his "remarkable quiet insight" from her. Emily Dickinson says he was right about all the persons he wrote about and that they were all children compared to him, and when Sainte-Beuve accuses him of thinking he had improved upon him, he does not deny it, though still professing himself the Frenchman's pupil. Whistler tells William Morris Hunt that "there was a certain freshness about his manner that rather pleased me," but Hunt denies him art altogether. "All he has is a pale curiosity."[65] And so the debate continues.

All in all, perhaps we come as close as we can hope to a balance in his own remark to Lincoln: "No one can do my work as I should like to see it done, but I incline to feel that there are few who can do it better than I."[66] To which one might add this admission in a private letter: "I have always felt that what I did put of myself into my...books made a good deal of such attraction as they had for the readers who relished them."[67]

But what of praise and blame from others? Like Dickens, Bradford had a tendency to remember all the harsh things said of him rather than the praise and therefore avoided reading reviews except when he had arranged for them. He planned to drop the *Saturday Review of Literature* into the waste basket for two months to obviate the possibility of encountering an unfavorable review of *As God Made Them*, and he burned an *Atlantic* because he feared Henry Fairfield Osborn's review of *Darwin* would be unfavorable, after which, of course, a loving friend told him it was. Bliss Perry made him feel foolish as a writer and Katharine Lee Bates as a scholar, and he was capable of composing both an unfavorable review and a letter of rejection from Greenslet as literary exercises. Once, indeed, the *New York Times Book Review* praised him in terms "too extravagant even for my exaggerated sense of my own merits,"[68] yet when William Lyon Phelps, in a favorable review, tactlessly remarked that he had everything but genuis, the remark rankled, and he quoted it again and again.

The cruelest reviews Bradford ever received were Mark Van Doren's of *The Soul of Samuel Pepys*, with its complaint of his "fatuous familiarity," H. W. Boynton's of *The Haunted Biographer* under the heading "Squeaks and Gibbers," and Percy H. Boynton's devastating analysis of his style in *More Contemporary Americans*, of which The University of Chicago Press had the gall to invite him to purchase a copy. In all three cases, he wrote to the writers, admitting the justice of their complaints and telling them they had helped him, though his letters to others about them are rather different in tone. Percy Boynton, at least, seems to have been genuinely touched by his humility.[69] Harriet Monroe, rejecting verses he had submitted to *Poetry*, criticized what she called his clichés, and though he resented it, he thought she was right and told her so.

There is inevitably a certain slight suggestion of toadying about such letters; in fact he himself writes, "I am particularly anxious to make a good impression on [Stuart] Sherman and it is one of the great ambitions of my life to overcome the prejudices of the

Van Dorens."[70] But there can be no question as to his entire sincerity in his response to Barrett Wendell's letter about *A Prophet
of Joy*, which, though not entirely favorable, was so "wonderful . . .
in its sympathy, its graceful and really kindly tact," and had such
beauty and kindness and sweetness in its expression that he was
deeply moved. His most violent reaction to criticism was directed
at a publisher's reader who found the story of *Her Own Way* futile
and the characters unconvincing. "I hope that when this woman
gets to hell and offers the most ingenious plea she has to escape
damnation, the authorities there will blandly tell her that it is not
convincing." Yet, for all that, he still had an uneasy feeling that
she might be right: "I take human beings to pieces well enough.
Apparently I cannot put them together."[71]

Although Bradford sometimes felt that all his admirers were
women, ministers, or lunatics, praise from any source was welcome
to him. One day was brightened for him when a girl in Melrose
wrote to ask for an autograph, which he promptly sent, and it must
have been sweet to receive a letter from a stenographer who offered
to give him her Saturday afternoons free, being sure "that the bene-
fits I would derive from the association would more than repay
me."[72] When *The Truth Seeker* abused his psychograph of Tom
Paine, he sent them a conciliatory letter which made them more
friendly, and when a Catholic reader was offended by one of his
poems, he sent *Unmade in Heaven*. But of course it was best of all
when somebody like Chester Greenough "told his class that it was
fortunate for American literature that Gamaliel Bradford was still
alive and writing."[73]

The Sweet Smell of Success

In his early days, Bradford expressed a noble disdain for money,
but later he became much more interested in finance, devoting the
first days of each month to his accounts: "I love to turn over the
pages of my ledger, as the miser of old loved to turn over his bags.
A quarter of a million between me and poverty."[74] Until 1924 he
put himself through agony once a year, struggling with his income-

tax returns; then he turned the job over to an accountant, who found him $1,600 overpaid and recovered the amount.

As late as 1920, however, he earned only between $400 and $500 from his books, and in 1929 he estimated that during the forty years he had been writing he had probably earned less than $40,000 in all. After the success of *Damaged Souls* in 1923 and the large sums paid not only to writers like Strachey but even to his friend Howe, he became much more concerned about his earnings. He tried a number of agents, none of whom ever sold anything for him, especially in negotiations with the mass circulation magazines, and pondered all kinds of possible and impossible projects. In 1924, with *Bare Souls* coming out, *Her Own Way* being serialized, and "A Duchess of Dreams" in the hands of Jane Cowl, he pictured himself as the author of the year's best-selling novel and the best-selling work of nonfiction while his play was packing them in on Broadway. It was all perfect Walter Mitty, except that he was entirely aware of its absurdity.

The same fantastic honesty that appeared in his income-tax operations manifested itself again in his dealings with publishers. He would not accept an advance nor sign a contract for a book not yet written. Even while he dreamed of fantastic successes, he was sure that the book about to be published would fail and quite capable of telling the publisher so. More than once he offered to cancel a contract, though the other party had given no indication of such desire. When the Yale University Press proposed exempting 500 copies of *Shadow Verses* from royalty, he suggested that they pay no royalties at all until they had recovered expenses, and he once shocked Ferris Greenslet by proposing a greater reduction in royalties than the publisher had suggested. He must have shocked the agent Ann Watkins, too, by sending her 10 percent of what the *Delineator* had paid him for his paper on Madame de Sévigné (she said that only three authors had behaved thus in fifteen years' experience and that she thought better of human nature for it, but she kept the check), and he even offered to release the magazine from the obligation to pay for an article in which they had obviously been disappointed.

Nevertheless he did enjoy his late and hard-earned success. It was music to his ears to hear himself described as America's foremost biographer and to have Florence Converse write in the *Atlantic* that "a portrait by Bradford is coming to have as distinctive a connotation as a portrait by Sargent."[75] In April 1924, as he reported to Katharine Lee Bates, he was in *Harper's*, the *Atlantic*, the *American Mercury*, the *Forum*, the *North American Review*, the *Sewanee Review*, the *Literary Review*, the *Bookman*, and the *Lyric*. Publishers who had ignored him for years were contending for him. Macmillan wanted a life of Poe, Boni and Liveright a two-volume Washington, Doubleday a Lincoln. To Harpers he quoted Shakespeare and John Gay: "I am not worth the coil that's made for me" and "How happy could I be with either,/Were t'other dear charmer away." When, in September 1923, Houghton Mifflin feared losing him, they guaranteed a sale of 10,000 *Damaged Souls* by the first of the year. The Munsey interests offered $10,000 for a life of Frank Munsey. In addition to all this, there were all sorts of invitations for public appearances if only he had been well enough to accept them.

The Seattle Public Library and the American Club in Shanghai asked for autographed photographs. ("When I had looks, nobody wanted my photograph. Now that the inside is all that counts, they begin to get interested in the outside.")[76] He was interviewed and photographed for the *Boston Herald* and *Globe* and mentioned twice in one issue of the *Evening Transcript*. Greenslet phoned on a Sunday night to ask if they might put *Darwin* on the fall list, the *Herald* boomed the Coolidge article on the front page, and Rupert Hughes went all out for *Daughters of Eve*. Roger Babson brought him a book inscribed "To Gamaliel Bradford, whom all Wellesley loves, all America knows, and all the world reads," a man stopped his car and got out to shake hands "with one of our greatest writers," and "almost every day some one wants me to autograph a book, which has not yet ceased to be a pleasure and becomes a burden, though I could dispense with the bother of doing them up."[77]

The most undesirable element in his celebrity was that publishers were forever sending him all kinds of books for his opinion, and he would take time to look them over and write about them in a surprisingly large number of cases. His fantastic honesty remained unimpaired; as late as 1927 he told a young interviewer that both *Harper's* and the *Atlantic* had just refused articles, and Ferris Greenslet was driven to exasperation by his always thinking that his current book was not selling and was therefore a disappointment to the publishers. When he wanted to ward off a publisher, he could still do it very effectively by offering him one of his unpublished novels. Nor had the breed of idiots died out, and the editor of a verse magazine could write to suggest "that if I will pay the one dollar and a half subscription to her paper, I may have free revision of my poems and one published every month. She hopes I will send something, as she hears that I write very well."[78]

Beyond

But there was one overwhelming interest in Bradford's life that had nothing directly to do with literature—religion. He grew up "under a regime of strict Episcopalian orthodoxy," and though he thought his father's adherence to it pretty formal, his Aunt Sarah's was earnest in the extreme. In 1881 he records going to church to set a good example and because Christianity satisfied the religious needs of many people, though he himself had ceased to believe in it. But there are many 1883 entries in his journal which indicate anything but a settled unbelief. "We true Christians" think of God as "that nameless ever-present sense of power, above, around, beneath us, without and within ourselves, all-embracing."[79] Though he has some difficulty deciding whether he is a Christian, he is clearly reluctant to give up the name. "Why do we quarrel about our religion? is not God good, and is not nature beautiful?"[80] "Every tree, every cloud, every breath of air makes my heart leap with joy that I live, brings me nearer and nearer to God."[81] Contemplating the beauty of nature, he can write, "Then the Spirit of all, the Holy Ghost, descends upon me and lifts me to the seventh heaven, and brings me to gaze upon the wonder and majesty of the Eternal,"[82] which would seem to indicate a capacity for mystical experience one would not suspect from his later utterances. Yet when he and Helen Ford married, they felt they must give up church because the church did not foster the spiritual life, and in after years he believed this had been a great struggle for her and reproached himself for having encouraged it. He may well have been right, for Mrs. Bradford returned to churchgoing after his death.

Bradford's own skepticism always steered a clear course away from both atheism and agnosticism. He denied nothing, not even the possibility that others might know what he did not know, always maintaining that those who denied were quite as hopelessly enslaved to dogma as those who affirmed. He faced the formidable H. L. Mencken himself on this issue, and the fulminations of Harry Elmer Barnes sickened him. "You must have more confidence in your reason than I have," he wrote one correspondent, "to deny immortality absolutely. What is the use of a pretty complete skepticism if it does not allow you to hope for anything you wish?"[83] In some ways, this had its disadvantages. Bradford did not positively deny even hell, nor the possibility of his going there. But on the whole, hope seems to have prevailed. "I trust the Lord will temper the spiritual atmosphere to the aged goat as well as the shorn lamb, and it is possible that in heaven even I might enjoy myself."[84] He even felt that "somewhere, somehow, sometime, there would be another renaissance of the spiritual which would overcome the world as Christianity did two thousand years ago."[85]

The ideal of the Roman Catholic Church made a profound appeal to him, and for several years he attended Mass. But when he went to Italy, he thought the Roman priests lacked "not only all semblance of spiritual life but even of decent humanity," and he did not believe that "a religion which can produce or which can even tolerate such representatives" could ever content him.[86] Even at home he believed the Irish Catholics had turned Boston into "a slave-city" in which anybody who dared criticize them could count upon stirring up "a frenzy of tomcats," and when Al Smith ran for President, he practically went into hysterics. He had no faith whatever in the toleration of the Church. "It would burn you and me at the stake tomorrow, if it could, to save our souls. The whole of South America is a living witness of what we shall be taking a step toward if we elect Al Smith." For once he was tempted to follow in his father's footsteps, speaking out on a public issue, but he could not feel confident enough to court martyrdom. "After all, I am not sure of Catholicism any more than about anything else."[87]

The strangest thing about Bradford's religious struggles is that he should have identified the cause of religion in the world not only with Christian orthodoxy but with what we now call Fundamentalism. When Katharine Lee Bates found D. L. Moody a subject unworthy of his powers, he told her that "the Fundamentalist interpretation of Christianity was the only one that had really counted for much in the great development of the past" and that "modernist views of progressive Christianity" were mere "milk and water."[88] He spells this notion out in more detail in a review of Giovanni Papini's *Life of Christ*, a hopelessly inferior book by any standard. "Christ's," he declares, was "the life that has done more to transfigure the world than any other that has been known," and what he did for mankind was done "as God and not as man"; it was "the divine personality made flesh, knowing all the weakness of earth and pouring upon it all the strength of heaven" that had "really taken hold of agony and sin and sorrow." Papini "would say farther, and many of us will agree with him, that if the twentieth century is to be redeemed by Christianity, it can only be by the Christianity of Christ." And since the historical Jesus cannot be recovered, he praises the Italian writer for ignoring all the criticism which has subjected him to "a process of attenuation, explaining away, lopping off, cutting down this attribute, reducing that, till there was nothing left but the pale shadow of New England Unitarianism."[89]

To be sure, there are times when Bradford seems to catch a glimpse of something larger than this. Both William James and Matthew Arnold might have accepted his definition of God as "that something without which the human spirit can never be at rest."[90] Or, more elaborately, "The truth must be, I think, that God is our name for whatever gives reality to this vast elusive world of appearances and dreams. We seek and grope and shudder through it, and when we seem to put our fingers on something solid and enduring, we call it—God."[91] In *The Quick and the Dead*, he calls religion "the love of God, the need of God, the longing for God, and the constant sense of another world than this."[92] He also states repeatedly that the heart of religion is mysticism, and he must have known that the mystical experience is not to be identified with, and is not dependent upon, the theology of any particular religion. Yet in practice he completely dismissed both the religious value and the utility not only of Christian modernism but of the Judaism out of which Christianity developed as well as all other pre-Christian and non-Christian religions.

What must never be forgotten in considering Bradford's religious attitude, however, is that it was his considered view that without God there is no meaning and no comfort in life. The religious hunger of Don Marquis was what impressed him most in reading his *Poems and Portraits*, and when Marquis admitted that he had read him aright, he wrote, "As to God, the subject is inexhaustible. I have been at it for forty years; but I don't get anywhere, and the flesh is worn off my bones and bloom off my soul in the effort."[93]

Yet, from another point of view, Bradford did not work at it. In 1918 he writes that he has not prayed for thirty-five years, and he engaged in no other religious exercises either. He would probably have taken a dim view of Mary Austin's saying that the most important thing about a religion was not to believe in it but to practice it. After his sister-in-law had been converted in the good old Fundamentalist way, he told her he did not wish to be. "Pride . . . is my great vice, intellectual pride, and I could not bear the thought of giving up my own will, my own way, of accepting a master, or becoming a follower or servant."[94] In his journal he preserves the rejected ending for Chapter 2 of the Moody, in which he asks himself whether he would accept salvation on Moody's terms. He recognizes that the will to believe can accomplish anything and quotes Marlowe's "See how Christ's blood streams in the firmament" as summing up Moody's appeal. Then he writes:

Could that blood cleanse, purify, sanctify, transform, transfigure me?

Yet even as I write the words, I realize that the effort to make them clever means more to me than the blood of Christ. All the same, if D. L. Moody, or anybody else, could have given me God crucified in Christ Jesus, it would have changed my life.[95]

This of course was what fascinated him in Moody and made his work on the religious trilogy the great writing adventure of his life. "Really, until I began to meditate upon this matter, I hardly realized how intensely religion has always preoccupied my thought and my life, and now it seems as if there were no end to the thoughts and ideas and experiences that I have to pour out."[96] He was puzzled by the attraction of clergymen to him, yet somehow he could never get over wondering whether he ought not to have been a clergyman himself. In the dialogue he wrote for himself and Anatole France, he gives France the credit (or the blame) for much of his skepticism, but he also says that something in France repelled him and turned him to Lemaître. "I think he, like me, had an inborn, unquenchable craving for God and all that God stands for."[97] Certainly no reader of Bradford's books can ever have doubted the depth and sincerity of his response to both religion and piety in his subjects. He was shocked when a girl told him she had no belief in immortality and when he learned that a servant's child had not been taught to pray. In a dialogue between Ambrose White Vernon and his Aunt Sarah, he makes Vernon, who had a clerical background, tell her that Bradford is a better Christian than he is; in another, between Aunt Sarah and Harriet Cutler, Harriet admits that though he is a skeptic, he is really "a humble skeptic, an earnest seeker," and above all, gentle, always gentle, underneath"; in still another, between himself and Lee, he tells the general how bad he feels "because I have lost God, but I simply can't find him," to which Lee replies, "If I were you, I wouldn't try too hard. It seems to me that you live too hard in every way. Let the desire for God flow easily into your life, as it so manifestly flows into your books. He is everywhere. You cannot escape him."[98] But perhaps the most cogent word of all is the quotation he was fond of making from the Confederate vice-president, Alexander H. Stephens: "God may send me to hell, but if he does, he will be sending there the best friend he has in this world."[99]

In his preface to Bradford's *Journal*, Van Wyck Brooks spoke of "a literary life impressive in its devotion and continuity, a life which, in its steady integrity, its adaptation of means to valuable ends, its coherence and well-directed intensity, recalls the classical age of American letters." Taking into consideration the handicaps under which Bradford labored, one might add that it was also an heroic life. His idiosyncrasies harmed only himself; if in his journals and his "Autobiography" he made a habit of selling himself short by emphasizing and often exaggerating all the limitations which most of us do our best to excuse and to conceal, he not only stands clear of having inflicted them upon others, but so conducted himself that his fellows never even suspected their existence. One might well apply to him what he said of Mark Twain, that his faults were incidental to humanity and that as an individual he stood with the best. He left a shelf of sensitive, penetrating, humane, and aspiring books behind him, and his memory has been cherished by all who had the good fortune to know him.

Notes and References

All the manuscripts referred to are in the Houghton Library, Harvard University. To distinguish them from published works, these titles are placed within quotation marks.

Chapter One

1. "Journal," December 14, 1924.
2. "Journal," June 27, 1921.
3. GB to Miss Jordan, October 8, 1922. "Letter Books," 13:115.
4. GB to Marvin Sprague, December 8, 1919. "Letter Books," 2:150.
5. GB to Barrett H. Clark, April 8, 1930. "Letter Books," 47:191–92.
6. GB to Harriet Ford Cutler, October 14, 1883. "Letters to Harriet Ford Cutler," 1:141–43.
7. GB to Louis Feipel, July 21, 1923. "Letter Books," 7:172–73.
8. "Journal," March 20, 1920.
9. "Early Journal," October 4, 13, 1883.
10. "Journal," October 2, 1930.
11. "Journal," September 14, 1922.
12. GB to A. F. Hunter, January 5, 1930. *The Letters of Gamaliel Bradford* (Boston, 1934), pp. 331–32.
13. *Modern Language Notes* 25 (1910):51–56. See also GB's letters to E. H. O. Oliphant, August 24, 1919, and to Garland Greever, September 1, 1919, "Letter Books," 2:7–10 and 2:26. On June 12, 1922, GB wrote Lytton Strachey that the *Cardenio* study interested him more than any other literary work he had done, "Letter Books," 12:36–38. Bradford's scrapbook in Houghton contains a clipping of a letter

written to the *Nation*, May 31, 1905, in which he reasonably suggests *The Old Law*, attributed to Massinger, Middleton, and Rowley, as the source of Trollope's *The Fixed Period*.

14. GB to Alfred C. Potter, December 15, 1925. "Letter Books," 29:230–32. Cf. "Italian Journal," p. 1.

15. "Journal," March 25, 1927.

16. "Journal," October 2, 1925.

17. "Journal," April 22, 1927.

18. *D. L. Moody, A Worker in Souls* (New York, 1927), pp. 143–44.

19. "Italian Journal," January 13, 1887.

20. GB to Harriet Ford Cutler, March 29, 1896. "Letters to Harriet Ford Cutler," 2:1–2.

21. GB to Garland Greever, August 5, 1921. "Letter Books," 7:130–33.

22. "Journal," December 30, 1922; August 24, 1924; January 29, 1931.

23. "The High School Fifty Years Ago," in "Editorials and Reviews, 1928–29," pp. 143–44.

24. GB to John A. Berger, April 22, 1929. "Letter Books," 43:98. GB to M. R. Werner, January 21, 1920. "Letter Books," 46:165–66.

25. GB to E. K. Rand, December 20, 1925. "Letter Books," 29:238.

26. GB to John Macrae, March 31, 1927. "Letter Books," 35:77–78.

27. GB to Julia C. Harris, February 20, 1925. "Letter Books," 26:87.

28. When Archibald Henderson asked GB to name "the twelve most important personalities in the world today," the two writers he nominated were Shaw and Edgar Guest. Under *Athletes* he listed Lindbergh (heaven only knows why) and Babe Ruth. GB to Archibald Henderson, July 7, 1927. "Letter Books," 36:4–5.

29. "Journal," October 27, 1928.

30. GB to Bliss Perry, September 25, 1931. "Letter Books," 53:209.

31. GB to C. Alphonso Smith, February 25, 1921. "Letter Books," 7:1–2.

32. "Journal," May 26, 1929.

33. "Journal," May 21, 1930.

34. "Journal," August 20, 1926.

35. "Journal," June 15, 1930.

36. GB to M. A. DeWolfe Howe, January 19, 1921. "Letter Books," 6:137.

37. GB to A. Page Cooper, April 10, 1928. "Letter Books," 37:235.

38. GB to Harriet Monroe, March 12, 1922. "Letter Books," 10:186–87.

39. "Journal," November 2, 1919. GB to Stanley Rinehart, March 22, 1927. "Letter Books," 35:53.

40. "Journal," July 25, 1923.

41. "Journal," August 20, 1927; September 17, 1927.

42. GB to James Monahan, October 4, 1929. "Letter Books," 45:83. GB to A. Page Cooper, December 16, 1928. "Letter Books," 41:196–97.

43. GB to John Farrar, February 25, 1929. "Letter Books," 42:140–41.

Chapter Two

1. *A Pageant of Life* (Boston, 1904).

2. *Shadow Verses* (New Haven, 1920).

3. GB to H. L. Mencken, January 28, 1921. "Letter Books," 6:160.

4. "Journal," May 13, 1922.

5. "The Spelling Book," "Poems," 6:59.

6. "Hope," "Poems," 3:49.

7. "H.F.B., May 11, 1928," "Poems," 9:3.

8. "Poems," 1:2.

9. "The Charm," "Poems," 2:143.

10. "The Assignation," "Poems," 2:27.

11. "Rest," "Poems," 2:40.

12. "Disaster," "Poems," 3:25.

13. "The Appeal," "Poems," 2:64.

14. "Virtue," "Poems," 5:148.

15. "Long Ago," "Poems," 2:58.

16. "All Over," "Poems," 3:29.

17. *Shadow Verses*, p. 80.

18. *Shadow Verses*, p. 81.

19. *A Prophet of Joy* (Boston, 1920), p. 1.

20. GB to William Lyon Phelps, October 15, 1918. "Letter Books," 1:12–14.

21. GB to Ellery Sedgwick, June 28, 1919. *Letters*, pp. 8–9.

22. GB to Barrett Wendell, August 30, 1920. *Letters,* pp. 40–41.

23. GB to M. A. DeWolfe Howe, July 3, 1919. "Letter Books," 1:157.

24. "Journal," July 1, 1920.

25. GB to Garland Greever, February 17, 1923. "Letter Books," 15:137–39.

26. "Journal," March 7, 1922.

27. "Journal," July 9, 1916.

28. "Journal," June 28, 1930.

29. "Journal," August 12, 1920.

30. GB to Harriet Monroe, October 20, 1921. "Letter Books," 8:57. Cf. December 12, 1921 (8:165), and her reply (8:187).

31. "Exquisite," "Poems," 10:17.

Chapter Three

1. In a "Journal" entry, August 18, 1919, Bradford listed his Fools: Henry Clifford in "Girard," Maurice Dearborn in "Tennis Balls," Charlie Perkins in "The Crackling of Thorns," Maurice Lamont in "Autumn Love," Gilbert Walden in *Her Own Way,* Gordon in *The Private Tutor,* Bryan Lafarge in "Mamma," Egbert Warren in "Charm," Fergus Clay in "Who Pays?" Bill in *A Prophet of Joy,* and Flitters in *Matthew Porter* and "The Secret of Woodbine Lodge." He added that there were no real female clowns, the closest approaches being Flora Chantrey in *Matthew Porter,* Kitty in "Woodbine Lodge," Lillian in "Mamma," and Jeannette in *Her Own Way.* In a prefatory note to "Girard," he adds the Clown in "A Mad World" and the Young Poet in "A Love Knot," but in a note added to his "Journal" entry for December 23, 1919, he says he did not definitely think of the type until "A Mad World" (1888) or of a modern form before conceiving *A Prophet of Joy,* Henry Clifford being only an anticipation, vaguely based on Shelley.

2. *Unmade in Heaven* (New York, 1917), p. vii.

3. GB to Edward Wagenknecht, December 21, 1927. "Letter Books," 38:133.

4. GB to Edward Wagenknecht, November 30, 1930. "Letter Books," 50:115–17.

5. GB to Garland Greever, November 26, 1921. "Letter Books," 8:133.

6. "Journal," February 3, 1931.
7. "Journal," September 9, 1931.

Chapter Four

1. Prefatory note to "Girard."
2. "Journal," July 3, 1926.
3. "Journal," May 16, 1922.
4. *The Private Tutor* (Boston, 1904), pp. 223, 237, 13, 200, 74.
5. *Between Two Masters* (Boston, 1906), p. 331.
6. "Journal," June 15, 1919.
7. *Matthew Porter* (Boston, 1908), p. 155.
8. In "Editorials and Reviews, 1921–23," pp. 55–57, we have the beginning of a rather promising short story, "Blim," which Bradford marked "Given up because of the close similarity to Mackay's [i.e. Mac-Kaye's] Dogtown Common." In a poor city flat, a child lies dying, attended, among others, by a social worker who gave up studying for the ministry because he feared he did not believe enough and Blim, a wild but loving chorus girl of unknown origin. The story ends as the two walk away together after the child's death, and the girl questions the man about God. As far as it goes, "Blim" has an excellent narrative style, and the dialogue is lifelike.
9. GB to Lyman Beecher Stowe, January 11, 1924. "Letter Books," 20:44–45.
10. "Journal," July 15, 1921.

Chapter Five

1. *Union Portraits* (Boston, 1916), p. ix.
2. "Journal," December 12, 1924.
3. GB to Edwin D. Starbuck, November 15, 1929. "Letter Books," 45:181–84.
4. "Journal," August 30, 1926.
5. "Biography and the Universe," in "Miscellaneous Essays."
6. GB to William Roscue Thayer, April 8, 1920, *Letters*, pp. 32–34.
7. GB to Lytton Strachey, November 2, 1922. "Letter Books," 13:186–89.
8. "Journal," September 5, 1926. See also GB to Ambrose W. Vernon, November 5, 1925. *Letters*, pp. 231–32.

9. GB to T. G. Noble, November 13, 1929. "Letter Books," 45: 171–73.

10. GB to Worthington C. Ford, February 24, 1925. "Letter Books," 26:97.

11. GB to Talcott Williams, July 7, 1919. "Letter Books," 1:160.

12. "Journal," June 20, 1927; December 2, 1929.

13. Wives (New York, 1925), pp. 128, 185.

14. Daughters of Eve (Boston, 1930), pp. 31–32, 51, 142, 197.

15. "Journal," June 12, 1927. Cf. The Journal of Gamaliel Bradford (Boston, 1933), p. 318.

16. GB to Jean Maury, March 30, 1928. "Letter Books," 39:167–70.

17. "Journal," January 8, 1929.

18. GB to Ruth Mulligan, November 18, 1930. "Letter Books," 59:61–63.

19. "Journal," June 9, 1930.

20. "Journal," November 18, 1928.

21. Journal, p. 466. February 24, 1928.

22. This does not exhaust the subjects Bradford had in mind. He had completely outlined two books. The first was "Self-Dissectors," a book on the great diarists: "A Judge Self-Judged: Samuel Sewall, The Secrets of a Saint: John Wesley, The Lining of a President: John Quincy Adams, The Soul of a Singer: Thomas Moore, The Bubble of Life: Amiel, Souls in Gaul: The Goncourts, The Diary of a Disappointed Man: Barbellion."

The other was "Creation," the book on great artists which he was all ready to set to work on when he died, with Tasso's "There is no real creator save God and the artist" as its epigraph: "The Splendor of Creation: Leonardo da Vinci, The Triumph of Creation: Benvenuto Cellini, The Struggle of Creation: Ludwig van Beethoven, The Despair of Creation: Benjamin Robert Haydon, The Business of Creation: Anthony Trollope, The Creatrix: Charlotte Cushman, The Process of Creation: William Morris Hunt."

The last two of these had been written some time before and were later included in Biography and the Human Heart. In 1928 Bradford even proposed to the Ladies' Home Journal a series of brief "fantastic or ironical" sketches of Grant, Coolidge, Mencken, S. Parkes Cadman, The Silent Woman, The Silent Policeman, The Enemy of Silence, and God, which might pass under the title "Studies in Silence." How serious he was about this and just what he meant by the more cryptic titles was best known to himself.

23. *Confederate Portraits* (Boston, 1914), pp. 106, 142, 213, 197; *Portraits of Women* (Boston, 1916), p. 115; *Union Portraits*, p. 5; *Damaged Souls* (Boston, 1923), p. 249; *As God Made Them* (Boston, 1929), p. 139.

24. *Portraits of Women*, p. 115; *Union Portraits*, pp. 229, 141, 193; *The Quick and the Dead* (Boston, 1931), p. 23; *Confederate Portraits*, p. 157.

25. *Wives*, p. 262.

26. *Union Portraits*, p. 255; *Wives*, pp. 188–89; *The Quick and the Dead*, pp. 64, 214.

27. *The Quick and the Dead*, pp. 18, 24.

28. "Journal," October 31, 1923.

29. *Journal*, p. 362. June 7, 1924.

30. "Journal," June 1, 1924, February 13, 1931.

31. GB to W. W. Keen, September 27, 1929. "Letter Books," 45:71.

32. "The Story of Life," in "Editorials and Reviews, 1929–30," pp. 1–5. Cf. "Collecting Souls," in "Editorials and Reviews, 1928–29," pp. 140–42.

33. "Journal," March 11, 1930. Cf. May 18, 1927.

34. GB to H. L. Mencken, October 15, 1930. "Letter Books," 49:195.

35. "Journal," March 23, 1925.

36. Bradford's most important discussions of psychography in print are "Psychography," in *A Naturalist of Souls*; "Lee and Psychography," in *Lee the American*; "A Clue to the Labyrinth of Souls," in *Bare Souls*; "Confessions of a Biographer," in *Wives*; and "Biography and Haystacks," in Edward Wagenknecht, *The Man Charles Dickens.* (Boston: Houghton Mifflin, 1929). In manuscript, see also "Psychography," in "Editorials and Reviews, 1921–23," pp. 191–96, and "Psychography, A Syllabus," in "Editorials and Reviews, 1923–24," pp. 127–34, which describes principles of research and draws up a list of important resources. "Biography and the Human Heart" and "Biography by Mirror" in *Biography and the Human Heart* (Boston, 1932), like "The Art of Biography," *Saturday Review of Literature* 1(1925):769–70, deal with biography in general rather than psychography in particular, as do the following items in "Editorials and Reviews" for the dates indicated:

"You and I and Biography," 1921–23, pp. 133–36; "Biography and Life," 1921–23, pp. 166–73; "The Material of Biography," 1928–29, pp. 111–13; and "Biography as a Fine Art," 1929–30, pp. 88–91.

Chapter Six

1. GB to Harold Latham, May 1922. "Letter Books," 10:168–69.
2. *A Naturalist of Souls* (Boston, 1926), p. 25.
3. *Union Portraits*, p. 78; *American Portraits, 1875–1900*, p. 27.
4. *Lee the American*, p. 37. Four years later, he reaffirmed this position in *Union Portraits*, pp. 101–102, though here admitting that "it may easily be maintained that one who followed a different course would show a broader, a more far-seeing, a more self-sacrificing patriotism, even as a New Englander." Yet, in the piece on "The Battle of Gettysburg," which he appended to *Confederate Portraits*, he makes it clear that he believed a Southern victory in the Civil War would have defeated the whole American experiment in government and been a lasting calamity for civilization.
5. *Confederate Portraits*, p. 253.
6. The 1926 edition of *Lee the American*, in which minor errors in the original edition were corrected, had a new preface, and there is a biographical paper on Lee in *Portraits and Personalities* (see Chapter 7, of the volume in hand). There are two other papers on Lee in "Editorials and Reviews, 1923–24": "The Place of Robert E. Lee in American History," an excellent mini-portrait (pp. 61–72), and "The Glory of Robert E. Lee" (pp. 169–72).
7. There is a brief paper on General Grant in "Editorials and Reviews, 1921–23," pp. 52–54.
8. *Union Portraits*, p. 99.
9. *Portraits of Women* (Boston, 1916), pp. ix–x.
10. "Journal," December 31, 1928.
11. A later portrait of Madame de Sévigné, structurally superior to the one in *Portraits of Women*, appeared in the *Delineator*, Vol. 109, November 1926.
12. *Portraits of American Women* (Boston, 1919), p. 101.
13. GB to Paul Reynolds, September 25, 1929. "Letter Books," 45:62.
14. GB to H. L. Mencken, July 19, 1921. "Letter Books," 8:93.
15. GB to Garland Greever, January 26, 1919. *Letters*, p. 4.

16. There is one slight suggestion (*Portraits of American Women,* pp. 201–202) of the lesbianism, either active or latent, suggested in Mary Earhart's later biography, *Frances Willard: From Prayer to Politics* (Chicago: University of Chicago Press, 1944), but there is no suggestion whatever that during her later years Miss Willard moved toward both socialism and religious eclecticism and began to lose faith in prohibition as the most effective solution to the alcohol problem.

17. An entry in Bradford's "Journal," May 25, 1924, indicates that at one time he considered including Mrs. Eddy, who had three husbands but whose claim to fame is certainly not as a wife. It is also true that though Theodosia Burr had a husband, she is much more interesting for her relationship to her father.

18. "Journal," September 8, 1924.

19. *Wives,* p. 19.

20. GB to Marvin Sprague, July 14, 1924. "Letter Books," 23:70–72.

21. Since there is no biography of Harriet Blaine, Bradford sent out a questionnaire to a number of persons who knew her. The results were quite unsatisfactory, the replies being either too general to be worth anything or so contradictory that they canceled each other out. Mrs. Blaine was obviously a very positive and to some an abrasive personality who called out very different responses from different people. "I do not think I shall again try the experiment." "I feel safer in relying upon the evidence of the letters, unimpeachable so far as it goes." *Wives,* pp. 245–46. For further comment on Abigail Adams, Peggy Arnold, Theodosia Burr, Varina Davis, Harriet Blaine, and Sarah Butler, see "Women in American History," in "Editorials and Reviews, 1921–23," pp. 128–31.

22. "Journal," December 21, 1927.

23. "Journal," March 18, 1929.

24. "Journal," April 17, 1928.

25. Bradford's *Elizabethan Women* (Boston, 1936) was written between 1890 and 1910 but not published until four years after his death. It is not psycography and is mentioned here because it is the only other book of Bradford's devoted to women. After a general introduction on "Elizabethan England," we find, in Part I, three chapters on "The Daily Life of Elizabethan Women"—educational, domestic, and social. Part II concerns "The Women of Elizabethan Literature." After a general first chapter, we have, in order, the women of Dekker and Hey-

wood, Middleton and Webster, Beaumont and Fletcher, Massinger and Ford, and "Shirley and Others." The last two chapters are "The Serpent of Old Nile: A Study of the Cleopatra of Tragedy" and "The Women of 'The Fairy Queen.'" The book shows an easy command of the knowledge of its time of composition in the field of the Elizabethan drama and, to a lesser extent, Elizabethan life, plus a skill in presenting these matters in a nontechnical style which ought to have appealed to a reasonably wide public.

26. GB to Garland Greever, September 23, 1920. "Letter Books," 5:76.

27. GB to Ellery Sedgwick, May 4, 1920. "Letter Books," 3:196–97.

28. GB to Josephine Peck, July 21, 1929. "Letter Books," 44:88–89.

29. GB to A. W. Vernon, March 1, 1925. "Letter Books," 26:119–21.

30. *Journal*, p. 321. September 11, 1922.

31. "Journal," March 13, 1924.

32. GB to Lee Foster Hartman, November 25, 1924, "Letter Books," 25:52–54.

33. GB to H. L. Mencken, November 6, 1924. "Letter Books," 24:241.

34. "Journal," November 17, 1924.

Chapter Seven

1. *Damaged Souls* (1923), pp. 3–4.

2. "Journal," June 5, 1922.

3. GB to Ellery Sedgwick, November 23, 1922. "Letter Books," 23:66–67.

4. GB to Garland Greever, November 18, 1922. "Letter Books," 14:58–59.

5. GB to Lyon G. Tyler, March 10, 1923. "Letter Books," 16:26–27.

6. "Journal," 9:21–22.

7. "Journal," July 18, 1921.

8. GB to George D. Seymour, November 27, 1922. "Letter Books," 14:82.

9. GB to Jessie B. Buford, January 1, 1923. "Letter Books," 15:72. GB to Henry B. Stevens, January 4, 1923. "Letter Books," 14:187.

10. GB to Lee Foster Hartman, August 26, 1922. "Letter Books," 12:16. *Journal*, p. 317. August 27, 1922.

11. GB to Lee Foster Hartman, June 10, 1923. "Letter Books," 17:62.

12. GB to Jessie P. Buford, July 1923. "Letter Books, 17:170–71.

13. *The Soul of Samuel Pepys* (Boston. 1924), pp. 238–39.

14. *Bare Souls* (New York, 1924).

15. *Saints and Sinners* (Boston, 1932).

16. "Journal," October 22, 1920.

17. "Journal," September 9, 1931.

18. GB to Garland Greever, February 20, 1931. "Letter Books," 51:104–106.

19. "Journal," January 4, 1932.

20. GB to A. W. Vernon, November 27, 1930. "Letter Books," 50:9709.

21. GB to F. L. Allen, January 15, 1931. "Letter Books," 50:226.

22. *Journal*, p. 534. October 25, 1931.

23. GB to Alfred Harcourt, October 14, 1925. "Letter Books," 29:39.

24. The modernists did not. A committee composed of Harry Emerson Fosdick, S. Parkes Cadman, Bishop Francis J. McConnell, and others chose the Moody as the first selection of the Religious Book Club, and Paul Moody, the evangelist's modernist son, praised it enthusiastically; see his letter to GB, August 30, 1927, "Letter Books," 36: 219–20. It seems odd, therefore, that Bradford should have written one correspondent that "the only friendly acceptance" had come from the orthodox. GB to Mrs. John D. Leitch, February 10, 1928, "Letter Books," 39:44–45.

25. GB to Garland Greever, June 14, 1925. "Letter Books," 27:129–31.

26. "Journal," July 4, 1925.

27. GB to Garland Greever, July 12, 1925. "Letter Books," 27:180–81.

28. GB to Garland Greever, March 11, 1926. "Letter Books," 30:186–88.

29. *D. L. Moody, A Worker in Souls* (New York, 1927), p. 39.

30. GB to Norreys O'Conor, August 9, 1921. "Letter Books," 8:141.

31. GB to W. W. Keen, September 12, 1922. "Letter Books," 13:47.

32. *Darwin* (Boston, 1926), p. 44.

33. "Journal," October 11, November 3, 9, 11, 1926.

34. "Journal," October 2, 3, 9, 1926.

35. *Life and I, An Autobiography of Humanity* (Boston, 1928), p. 4.

36. *The Quick and the Dead* (Boston, 1931).

37. "Journal," September 3, 1929.

38. "Journal," September 24, 25, 27, October 7, 12, 1929.

39. GB to Ellery Sedgwick, October 12, 1929. "Letter Books," 45:101.

40. GB to Virginia McCormick, August 5, 1930. "Letter Books," 48:245–46.

41. "Journal," September 11, 1928.

42. "Journal," March 5, 1930.

43. "Journal," April 22, 29, 1930.

44. "Journal," May 12, 1930.

45. "Journal," July 26, 1930.

46. "Journal," August 8, 1930.

47. GB to Willis J. Abbot, October 14, 1930. "Letter Books," 49:192.

48. E. M. House to GB, January 26, 1931. "Letter Books," 51:19; William E. Dodd to GB, January 29, 1931. "Letter Books," 51:42.

49. GB to F. W. Scott, May 30, 1931. "Letter Books," 52:134.

50. *Portraits and Personalities*, ed. Mabel A. Bessey (Boston, 1933).

51. GB to Edward Wagenknecht, February 19, 1925. "Letter Books," 26:82–83. Bradford's piece on Shakespeare has been reprinted in Wagenknecht's *The Personality of Shakespeare* (Norman: University of Oklahoma Press, 1972).

52. *The Haunted Biographer: Dialogues of the Dead* (Seattle, 1927). See also his "Little Glimpses of Great People," *Southwest Review*, Vol. 10, October 1924, pp. 40–48; "Little Glimpses of Great Men," *Sewanee Review* 32 (1924):176–79; "Glimpses of Great People," *Forum* 72 (1925):545–51. The *Boston Herald* material is preserved in manuscript in Bradford's five-volume "Editorials and Reviews" in the Houghton Library. If space had been available, the chapbook would have included two more sections, one centered around Isabel of Magny, heroine of "Ravenac," and a more miscellaneous "Books and Life"; the present writer has a copy of this material. The Houghton

Library also has a 101-page manuscript collection called "The Haunted Biographer," of which there is another copy in the writer's collection, and a great many more dialogues are scattered through the "Journal."

53. "Journal," January 6, 1928.

54. "Journal," August 30, 1931, September 8, 1931, October 4, 1931, September 10, 1925, November 11, 1924.

55. "Journal," February 21, 1925, November 1, 1930, April 6, 1923, June 6, 1922, August 31, 1930, July 31, 1926.

Chapter Eight

1. GB to Dorothy Whitney, January 28, 1930. "Letter Books," 46:196.

2. "Early Journal," 2:49. December 25, 1883.

3. GB to Garland Greever, December 16, 1928. "Letter Books," 41:193–94.

4. *Journal*, pp. 486–87, July 20, 1929.

5. *Journal*, p. 148, January 16, 1919; pp. 202–203, April 25, 1920.

6. GB to Garland Greever, July 8, 1923. *Letters*, pp. 141–43.

7. "Journal," February 28, 1927.

8. GB to Harriet Heiser, April 25, 1924. "Letter Books," 22:51–54.

9. "Journal," November 2, 1919.

10. "The Best of All," *Shadow Verses*, p. 17.

11. GB to Mr. Thomason, October 20, 1926. "Letter Books," 33:96.

12. *Portraits of Women*, pp. 141–42.

13. "Journal," April 7, 1929.

14. "Letters to Harriet Ford Cutler," 2:96–97, June 27, 1897.

15. GB to Garland Greever, December 24, 1922. "Letter Books," 14:154–55.

16. GB to Jessie P. Buford, December 16, 1930. "Letter Books," 50:156.

17. "Journal," January 12, 1918.

18. "The Humanity of Greatness," in "Editorials and Reviews, 1928–29," pp. 5–6.

19. GB to M. R. Werner, January 29, 1925. "Letter Books," 30:69–71.

20. "Journal," October 14, 1925.

21. *Journal*, p. 513, May 14, 1931.

22. "Journal," May 17, 1930.

23. "Journal," August 9, 1931.

24. GB to Harold DeWolf Fuller, September 2, 1930. *Letters*, pp. 41–43.

25. "Party," in "Editorials and Reviews, 1928–29," pp. 70–71.

26. GB to Loring A. Shuler, January 27, 1932. "Letter Books," 54:221.

27. *The Quick and the Dead*, p. 44.

28. "Editorials and Reviews, 1924–27," pp. 23–29.

29. "Journal," January 11, October 22, 1918.

30. GB to M. A. DeWolfe Howe, December 29, 1923. "Letter Books," 20:10. "Equality," in "Women and Other Things," pp. 144–45.

31. GB to Mark Van Doren, April 22, 1916. "Letter Books," 31:54.

32. "A Roof and a Bank-Book," in "Editorials and Reviews, December 1924–December 1927," pp. 67–68; "The Miracle of Civilization," in "Editorials and Reviews, 1928–29," pp. 54–56.

33. "Journal," August 4, 8, 1927; GB to Mr. King, December 13, 1928. "Letter Books," 41:184.

34. GB to Louis Untermeyer, February 28, 1923. "Letter Books," 15:183–85.

35. "Journal," February 14, 1929.

36. "Journal," January 31, 1918.

37. "Journal," November 28, 1925.

38. GB to Harriet Heiser, December 16, 1926. "Letter Books," 25:146–48.

39. "Early Journal," 2:125. March 20, 1884.

40. GB to Lee Foster Hartman, April 25, 1924. "Letter Books," 22:58.

41. "Sinful Kisses," in "Poems," 9:28.

42. "Journal," September 18, 1926.

43. "Journal," November 12, 1919.

44. "Journal," September 12, 1926.

45. "Journal," June 6, 1927.

46. "Duties of Suffrage," clipping in GB's scrapbook, Houghton.

47. "The Haunted Biographer," p. 65.

48. GB to Lawrence W. Lamm, November 21, 1930. "Letter Books," 50:69.

49. GB to Alice Brown, November 11, 1931. "Letter Books," 55:97.

50. GB to James E. Van Toor, January 6, 1931. "Letter Books," 50:194.

51. "Early Journal," 1:58 (March 3, 1883); 1:63 (March 11, 1883); 2:38 (December 13, 1883); 2:90 (February 8, 1884); 2:156 (May 2, 1884); 2:170 (May 28, 1884).

52. GB to H. L. Mencken, August 5, 1930. "Letter Books," 40:240.

53. "Journal," September 29, 1931.

54. GB to Garland Greever, August 19, 1923. "Letter Books," 17:62–64.

55. "Journal," August 7, 1929.

56. "Journal," January 10, 1928.

57. GB to Ellery Sedgwick, January 21, 1925. "Letter Books," 25:223–24.

58. "Journal," July 12, 1923. Cf. the more detailed accounts of his planning in *Journal*, pp. 386–87 (June 8, 1925) and 392 (July 30, 1925).

59. "Journal," August 2, 1930.

60. "Journal," February 19, 1922; October 6, 1923; September 2, 1925; December 28, 1928. GB to Marie Moloney, February 1, 1926. "Letter Books," 30:83–84.

61. "Journal," April 24, 1929.

62. "Journal," November 12, 1928.

63. "Journal," November 14, 1921; July 9, 1925.

64. "Journal," June 22, 1929.

65. "The Haunted Biographer," pp. 5, 39, 42, 52, 53, 77, 82–83.

66. "Journal," August 5, 1930.

67. GB to Annie Abbott, March 10, 1926. "Letter Books," 30:183.

68. "Journal," July 8, 1917.

69. GB to Mark Van Doren, May 21, 1924. "Letter Books," 22:175; cf. to Norreys O'Conor, June 3, 1924—22:185; to H. W. Boynton; January 6, 1928—38:166; to Julia C. Harris, January 6, 1928—38:167–68; to Virginia McCormick, February 16, 1928—39:75–76; to Percy H. Boynton, June 12, 1924—*Letters*, pp. 189–90.

70. "Journal," March 8, 1925.

71. "Journal," September 16, 1919.

72. "Journal," June 27, 1931.

73. "Journal," May 31, 1920.

74. "Journal," December 28, 1924.

75. "Journal," January 21, 1920.

76. GB to E. F. Edgett, November 3, 1922. "Letter Books," 13:190.

77. "Journal," July 10, 1931, April 22, 1930.

78. "Journal," July 2, 1929.

79. "Early Journal," 1:99. May 20, 1883.

80. "Early Journal," 1:83. May 24, 1883.

81. *Journal*, p. 33. July 2, 1883.

82. "Early Journal," 2:14. November 15, 1883.

83. GB to Eva H. Jeffers, February 18, 1931. "Letter Books," 51:91.

84. GB to Garland Greever, September 23, 1920. "Letter Books," 5:75.

85. GB to Thomas Roper, November 26, 1930. "Letter Books," 50:92–93.

86. "Journal," April 25, 1919. GB to J. Mack Williams, March 10, 1930. "Letter Books," 47:29–30.

87. "Journal," June 28, 1919, September 17, 1928. GB to M. A. DeWolfe Howe, September 10, 1928. "Letter Books," 40:167–68.

88. "Journal," July 10, 1935.

89. "Editorials and Reviews, 1921–1923," pp. 174–75.

90. *Saints and Sinners*, p. 219.

91. GB to J. R. Moseley, October 21, 1928. "Letter Books," 41:12.

92. *The Quick and the Dead*, p. 30.

93. GB to Don Marquis, March 9, 1922. "Letter Books," 10:181. The review of *Poems and Portraits* is in "Editorials and Reviews, 1921–1923," pp. 58–60; also "The Need of God," in "Editorials and Reviews, 1928–1929," pp. 124–26.

94. "Letters to Harriet Ford Cutler," 2:109–113. April 13, 1926.

95. "Journal," April 13, 1926.

96. "Journal," March 27, 1925.

97. "Journal," August 8, 1929.

98. "Journal," January 31, 1928; July 29, 1923; July 9, 1930.

99. GB to J. R. Moseley, June 1, 1926. "Letter Books," 31:153.

Selected Bibliography

PRIMARY SOURCES

1. Books

American Portraits, 1875–1900. Boston: Houghton Mifflin Company, 1922.

As God Made Them: Portraits of Some Nineteenth-Century Americans. Boston: Houghton Mifflin Company, 1929.

Bare Souls. New York: Harper and Brothers, 1924.

Between Two Masters. Boston: Houghton, Mifflin and Company, 1906.

Biography and the Human Heart. Boston: Houghton Mifflin Company, 1932.

Confederate Portraits. Boston: Houghton Mifflin Company, 1914.

Damaged Souls. Boston: Houghton Mifflin Company, 1923.

Darwin. Boston: Houghton Mifflin Company, 1926.

Daughters of Eve. Boston: Houghton Mifflin Company, 1930.

D. L. Moody: A Worker in Souls. New York: George H. Doran Company, 1927.

Early Days in Wellesley. Wellesley: The Wellesley National Bank, 1929.

Elizabethan Women. Edited by Harold Ogden White. Boston: Houghton Mifflin Company, 1936.

The Haunted Biographer: Dialogues of the Dead. Seattle: University Book Store, 1927.

The Journal of Gamaliel Bradford, 1883–1922. Edited by Van Wyck Brooks. Boston: Houghton Mifflin Company, 1933.

Lee the American. Boston: Houghton Mifflin Company, 1912.

The Letters of Gamaliel Bradford, 1918–1931. Edited by Van Wyck Brooks. Boston: Houghton Mifflin Company, 1934.

Life and I: An Autobiography of Humanity. Boston: Houghton Mifflin Company, 1928.

Matthew Porter. Boston: L. C. Page & Company, 1908.

A Naturalist of Souls: Studies in Psychography. New York: Dodd, Mead and Company, 1917. Revised Edition, Boston: Houghton Mifflin Company, 1926.

A Pageant of Life. Boston: Richard G. Badger, 1904.

Portraits and Personalities. Edited by Mabel A. Bessey. Boston: Houghton Mifflin Company, 1933.

Portraits of American Women. Boston: Houghton Mifflin Company, 1919.

Portraits of Women. Boston: Houghton Mifflin Company, 1916.

The Private Tutor. Boston: Houghton, Mifflin and Company, 1904.

A Prophet of Joy. Boston: Houghton Mifflin Company, 1920.

The Quick and the Dead. Boston: Houghton Mifflin Company, 1931.

Saints and Sinners. Boston: Houghton Mifflin Company, 1932.

Shadow Verses. New Haven: Yale University Press, 1920.

The Soul of Samuel Pepys. Boston: Houghton Mifflin Company, 1924.

Types of American Character. New York: The Macmillan Company, 1895.

Union Portraits. Boston: Houghton Mifflin Company, 1916.

Unmade in Heaven: A Play in Four Acts. New York: Dodd, Mead and Company, 1917.

Wives. New York: Harper and Brothers, 1925.

2. Manuscripts in the Houghton Library, Harvard University (fragments, preliminary drafts, and some brief items are not included in this list)

"Autumn Love" (novel)
"Bacchus and Ariadne" (play)
"Bags of Gold" (novelette)
"Bertha" (poem)
"The Bicycle Belles" (play)
"Charm" (play)
"The Crackling of Thorns" (play)

"The Crackling of Thorns" (novel)
"Death's Dainty Ways" (short story)
"A Duchess of Dreams" (play)
"Early Journal," 2 volumes
"Early Poems"
"Early Sketches of Percival"
"Editorials and Reviews," 5 volumes
"Elizabethan Lyrics" (criticism)
"An Elizabethan Mystic" (essay)
"The Flower of Love" (play for children)
"A Fool and Her Money" (play)
"Girard" (novel)
"The Gospel of Joy" (essays)
"The Haunted Biographer" (dialogues)
"A Humble Saint" (poem)
"Italian Journal"
"Journal," 23 volumes
"Letter Books," 56 volumes
"Letters of Gamaliel Bradford to Harriet Ford Cutler," 2 volumes
"Literature" (criticism)
"A Mad World" (play)
"Mamma" (play)
"Matthew Arnold" (essay)
"The Meteor" (short story)
"Miscellaneous Poems," 8 volumes
"Octaves" (poems)
"Poems," 10 volumes
"Ravenac" (play)
"The Reverend Arthur Meade" (novel)
"A Roman Holiday" (play)
"The Secret of Woodbine Lodge" (novel, also called "Madam Mystery")
"Shakespere, Bacon, and Common Sense" (essay)
"Short Essays"
"Success" (essay)
"Tennis Balls" (play, also called "Stella Brown")
"Verses Vain"
"Who Pays?" (play)
"Women and Other Things" (editorials)

3. Manuscripts in Wellesley College Library

"*The Wedding* and *The Young Admiral*, by James Shirley." Edited by
Gamaliel Bradford.

4. Selected, Uncollected Articles

"The Art of Biography." *Saturday Review of Literature* 1 (May 23,
1925):769–70.
"The Art of Psychography." *Literary Review* 3 (April 28, 1923):441–
42.
"Beaumont and Fletcher." *Atlantic Monthly* 101 (January 1908):126–
35.
"Browning and Sainte-Beuve." *North American Review* 191 (April
1910):488–500.
"Emerson." *New Princeton Review* 5 (March, 1888):147–63.
"Fiction as Historical Material." *Massachusetts Historical Society Pro-
ceedings* 48 (March 1915):326–32.
"The Fight for Glory." *Harper's Magazine* 159 (August 1929):309–15.
(Published anonymously. The original version, which was in-
tended to be signed, is in "Editorials and Reviews, 1926–29," pp.
174–90.)
"A French Critic of Old Imperialism." (Gaston Boissier.) *Atlantic
Monthly* 96 (December 1905):805–11.
"Glimpses of Great People." *Forum* 72 (April 1925):545–51.
"Her Own Way." *Stratford Monthly* 2 (August 1924):103–32; (Sep-
tember 1924):206–33; 3 (October 1924):14–36; (November
1924):107–33.
"The History of Cardenio by Mr. Fletcher and Shakespeare." *Modern
Language Notes* 25 (February 1910):51–56.
"Idealism in Literature." *Andover Review* 8 (November 1887):461ff.
"Journalism and Permanence." *North American Review* 202 (August
1915):239–41.
"Literature and Art." *Literary Review* 4 (August 2, 1924):929–30.
"Little Glimpses of Great Men." *Sewanee Review* 32 (July–September
1924):276–79.
"Little Glimpses of Great People." *Southwest Review* 10 (October
1924):40–48.
"The Mission of the Literary Critic." *Atlantic Monthly* 94 (October

1904):537–44.
"Nature in the Elizabethan Poets." *Poet-Lore* 7 (November 1895): 529–44.
"Sainte-Beuve and Biography." *Saturday Review of Literature* 7 (July 11, 1931):953–54.
"Santa Claus: A Psychograph." *Bookman* 62 (December 1925):403–406.
"A Sequel to the Iliad." *South Atlantic Quarterly* 10 (January 1911): 31–43.

SECONDARY SOURCES

Bolton, Charles K. "Gamaliel Bradford, A Memoir." *Massachusetts Historical Society Proceedings* 65 (1932–36):81–91. Charming, well-informed account by a friend, with emphasis on the man, not the work.
Capon, (Reginald) Laurence. "Gamaliel Bradford as Literary Critic, with Particular Reference to Elizabethan Drama." Ph.D. dissertation, Boston University, 1955. The only detailed study of Bradford's criticism; formulates general principles and proceeds to immensely detailed study of his application of them to Elizabethan writers.
Chase, William T., Jr. "Revelations of Gamaliel Bradford's Inner Personality Found in Pages of his Journals and Notebooks." *Boston Herald*, November 21, 1932. Includes quotations and interview with Mrs. Bradford.
Harris, Julia C. "An American Sainte-Beuve." *Emory University Quarterly* 4 (March 1948):16–21. Discursive comment by friend and admirer, with quotations from letters.
Howe, M. A. DeWolfe. "Gamaliel Bradford." In *Dictionary of American Biography*, First Supplement. New York: Charles Scribner's Sons, 1944. Standard, informed biographical summary.
Knickerbocker, Frances W. "Gamaliel Bradford Looks at His Art." *Sewanee Review* 42 (January–March 1934):90–99. Taking her point of departure from the *Journal*, Mrs. Knickerbocker achieves a searching, not always sympathetic, study.
Macy, John. "Gamaliel Bradford, Portrayer of Souls." *Bookman* 65

(May 1932):144–49. Memorial article by a distinguished critic. "Regarded totally, his work makes him the best biographer of our time. . . ."

Maikowski, Joseph Matthew. "Gamaliel Bradford, Psychographer." Ph.D. dissertation, University of Pittsburgh, 1924. Psychography in its relation to other forms of biography; comparison between Bradford and other character writers, with a whole chapter on Sainte-Beuve; critical examination of Bradford's psychographs; review of criticism.

McCormick, Virginia Taylor. "Bradford, Naturalist of Souls." *Personalist* 9 (January, 1928):27–37. Pleasant, not always completely accurate, commentary.

Murphy, Irene. "The Plays of Gamaliel Bradford in Relation to Some of his Other Work." Ph.D. dissertation, University of Kansas, 1953. Detailed study of Bradford's plays and their affinities.

Perrin, Marshall L. "Personal Tribute," *The Townsman* (Wellesley), April 15, 1932, p. 1. Reminiscences of Bradford's old tutor.

Urann, Margaret U. "Helen Ford Bradford Relates her Romance with Gamaliel," *The Townsman* (Wellesley), December 9, 1954, p. 16. This significant interview was given in 1946, on condition that the article should not be made public during Mrs. Bradford's lifetime.

Wagenknecht, Edward. "Our Editors: A Series of Studies, 3, Gamaliel Bradford," *Book League Monthly* 2, August, 1929, pp. 179–184. General consideration of psychography and Bradford's books, written to inform the members of the Book League, of which Bradford was an editor.

————. "Gamaliel Bradford, Psychographer," in Richard E. Langford and William H. Taylor, eds., *The Twenties: Poetry and Prose: 20 Critical Essays* (Deland, Florida: Everett Edwards Press, 1966), pp. 53–58. A similar study, written many years later for a more general audience.

Warren, Dale. "Gamaliel Bradford: A Personal Sketch," *South Atlantic Quarterly* 23 (January, 1933): 9–18. The author was Houghton Mifflin's publicity director while Bradford was publishing with them.

Woodruff, M. Dorothy. "Gamaliel Bradford, A Searcher of Souls," *South Atlantic Quarterly* 28 (October, 1929):419–28. General review with intelligent comment.

Index